BARRON'S BOOK NOTES

ERICH MARIA REMARQUE'S

All Quiet on the Western Front

BY

Rose Kam

SERIES EDITOR

Michael Spring
Editor, *Literary Cavalcade*
Scholastic Inc.

BARRON'S EDUCATIONAL SERIES, INC.
Woodbury, New York / London / Toronto / Sydney

ACKNOWLEDGMENTS

We would like to acknowledge the many painstaking hours of work Holly Hughes and Thomas F. Hirsch have devoted to making the *Book Notes* series a success.

All inquiries should be addressed to:
Barron's Educational Series, Inc.
113 Crossways Park Drive
Woodbury, New York 11797

Library of Congress Catalog Card No. 84-18402

International Standard Book No. 0-8120-3401-5

Library of Congress Cataloging in Publication Data
Kam, Rose.
    Erich Maria Remarque's All quiet on the western front.

    (Barron's book notes)
    Bibliography: p. 92
    1. Remarque, Erich Maria, 1898–1970. Im Westen nichts Neues. I. Title. II. Series.
PT2635.E68I68   1984   833'.912   84-18402
ISBN 0-8120-3401-5

PRINTED IN THE UNITED STATES OF AMERICA

456   550   98765432

CONTENTS

ADVISORY BOARD

We wish to thank the following educators who helped us focus our *Book Notes* series to meet student needs and critiqued our manuscripts to provide quality materials.

Murray Bromberg, Principal
Wang High School of Queens, Holliswood, New York

Sandra Dunn, English Teacher
Hempstead High School, Hempstead, New York

Lawrence J. Epstein, Associate Professor of English
Suffolk County Community College, Selden, New York

Leonard Gardner, Lecturer, English Department
State University of New York at Stony Brook

Beverly A. Haley, Member, Advisory Committee
National Council of Teachers of English Student
Guide Series, Fort Morgan, Colorado

Elaine C. Johnson, English Teacher
Tamalpais Union High School District
Mill Valley, California

Marvin J. LaHood, Professor of English
State University of New York College at Buffalo

Robert Lecker, Associate Professor of English
McGill University, Montréal, Québec, Canada

David E. Manly, Professor of Educational Studies
State University of New York College at Geneseo

Bruce Miller, Associate Professor of Education
State University of New York at Buffalo

Frank O'Hare, Professor of English
Ohio State University, Columbus, Ohio

Faith Z. Schullstrom, Member, Executive Committee
National Council of Teachers of English
Director of Curriculum and Instruction
Guilderland Central School District, New York

Mattie C. Williams, Director, Bureau of Language Arts
Chicago Public Schools, Chicago, Illinois

HOW TO USE THIS BOOK

You have to know how to approach literature in order to get the most out of it. This *Barron's Book Notes* volume follows a plan based on methods used by some of the best students to read a work of literature.

Begin with the guide's section on the author's life and times. As you read, try to form a clear picture of the author's personality, circumstances, and motives for writing the work. This background usually will make it easier for you to hear the author's tone of voice, and follow where the author is heading.

Then go over the rest of the introductory material—such sections as those on the plot, characters, setting, themes, and style of the work. Underline, or write down in your notebook, particular things to watch for, such as contrasts between characters and repeated literary devices. At this point, you may want to develop a system of symbols to use in marking your text as you read. (Of course, you should only mark up a book you own, not one that belongs to another person or a school.) Perhaps you will want to use a different letter for each character's name, a different number for each major theme of the book, a different color for each important symbol or literary device. Be prepared to mark up the pages of your book as you read. Put your marks in the margins so you can find them again easily.

Now comes the moment you've been waiting for—the time to start reading the work of literature. You may want to put aside your *Barron's Book Notes* volume until you've read the work all the way through. Or you may want to alternate, reading the *Book Notes* analysis of each section as soon as you have finished reading the corresponding part of the original. Before you move on, reread crucial passages you don't fully understand. (Don't take this guide's analysis for granted—make up your own mind as to what the work means.)

Once you've finished the whole work of literature, you may want to review it right away, so you can firm up your ideas about what it means. You may want to leaf through the book concentrating on passages you marked in reference to one character or one theme. This is also a good time to reread the *Book Notes* introductory material, which pulls together insights on specific topics.

When it comes time to prepare for a test or to write a paper, you'll already have formed ideas about the work. You'll be able to go back through it, refreshing your memory as to the author's exact words and perspective, so that you can support your opinions with evidence drawn straight from the work. Patterns will emerge, and ideas will fall into place; your essay question or term paper will almost write itself. Give yourself a dry run with one of the sample tests in the guide. These tests present both multiple-choice and essay questions. An accompanying section gives answers to the multiple-choice questions as well as suggestions for writing the essays. If you have to select a term paper topic, you may choose one from the list of suggestions in this book. This guide also provides you with a reading list, to help you when you start research for a term paper, and a selection of provocative comments by critics, to spark your thinking before you write.

THE AUTHOR AND HIS TIMES

Born Erich Paul Remark on June 22, 1898, he grew up in a Roman Catholic family in Osnabrück in the province of Westphalia, Germany—a city in the northwest part of what is now West Germany. He adored his mother, Anna Maria, but was never close to his father, Peter. The First World War effectively shut him off from his sisters, Elfriede and Erna. Peter Remark, descended from a family that fled to Germany after the French Revolution, earned so little as a bookbinder that the family had to move 11 times between 1898 and 1912. The family's poverty drove Remarque as a teenager to earn his own clothes money (giving piano lessons). He developed a craving for luxury, which he never outgrew. His piano playing and other interests, such as collecting butterflies and exploring streams and forests, later appeared in his fictional characters. His love of writing earned him the nickname Smudge.

Because of the frequent moving, Remarque attended two different elementary schools and then the Catholic Präparande (preparatory school). He loved the drama of Catholic rituals, the beauty of churches, the flowers in cloister gardens, and works of art. He later wrote with a sense of theater, and he featured churches and museums, flowers and trees as symbols of enduring peace. While in school, he had problems with teachers, however, and eventually paid them back by ridiculing them in his novels. At the Präparande he argued so much with one teacher that he used the man's personality and another's name (Konschorek) to produce a specific character in *All Quiet on the Western Front:* Schoolmaster Kantorek.

In November 1916, when Remarque was eighteen and a third-year student at Osnabrück's Lehrerseminar (teacher's college), he was drafted for World War I. After basic training at the Westerberg in Osnabrück (the Klosterberg of *All Quiet*), he was assigned to a reserve battalion, but often given leave to visit his seriously ill mother. In June 1917, he was assigned to a trench unit near the Western Front. He was a calm, self-possessed soldier, and when his classmate Troske was wounded by grenade splinters, Remarque carried him to safety. He was devastated when Troske died in the hospital of head wounds that had gone unnoticed. Still, he rescued another comrade before he himself was severely injured—also by grenade splinters—and sent to the St. Vincenz hospital in Duisburg for much of 1917–1918. He was there when his mother died in September 1917. A year later, still grieving for her, he returned to Osnabrück for further training. After the war he substituted her middle name, Maria, for his own, Paul.

The war ended before Remarque could return to active service, but even though he had not experienced frontline fighting at its worst, the war had changed his attitudes forever. He had learned to realize the value—and fragility—of each individual life, and had become disillusioned with a patriotism that ignored the individual. To him and many of his companions, civilian careers no longer held any meaning.

The next few years in Germany brought shortages, profiteering, runaway inflation, unemployment, riots, and extremist politics—including the rise of National Socialism from the postwar German Workers Party, a group almost fanatic in stressing nationalism. For lack of anything better to do, Remarque and several friends returned to the Seminar, but they found the studies and the older teachers' attitudes ridiculous. Remarque became involved in many disputes. For example, to ridicule the town authorities for their continued belief in the glory of war, he had himself photographed with his dog for the local paper—he in an officer's uniform decorated with two Iron Crosses and other medals. The scandalized Osnabrück officials demanded a public apology.

Still, at graduation he was given the customary letter of recommendation (although it did describe him as more freethinking than the average teacher), and in June 1919 he began two years' work as a substitute for teachers on leave. He was blond, strikingly good-looking, and very muscular, and managed to dress elegantly whatever his income. He stayed out of politics but became interested in all sports, especially cars and racing. Finally, bored with teaching, he wandered from job to job: playing organ on Sundays in an insane asylum, working for a tombstone firm, working as a small-town drama critic, writing advertising copy for an automotive firm. He married an actress, Jutta Ilse Zambona, in 1925, shortly after taking a job in Berlin as associate editor of the illustrated magazine, *Sport im Bild*, and became a regular in Berlin society, often sporting a monocle, superficially happy.

Early in 1920, as Erich Remark, he published a novel so poorly received that the embarrassment caused him to adopt his great grandfather's spelling of Remarque. His journalistic writing was still often mediocre and overly sentimental. Thus, the great success of his novel *All Quiet on the Western Front*, published in 1929, astonished him and everyone else. He hadn't even set out to write a bestseller but had written, instead, to rid himself of the bleak moods that he and his friends were still experiencing. "The shadow of war hung over us," he said, "especially when we tried to shut our minds to it." The result, known in German as *Im Westen nichts Neues*, deeply moved people on both sides of the Atlantic who were also still seeking to make sense of the war.

In its first year, German readers alone bought more than one million copies of *All Quiet*; and the British, French, and Americans bought thousands more. The novel also attained success as an American motion picture. (One of the first "talkies," the film, starring Lew Ayres and Lewis Wolheim, is still considered a classic. A 1979 made-for-television version starred Richard Thomas as Paul, Patricia Neal as Mrs. Bäumer, and Ernest Borgnine as Katczinsky.) By 1932 *All Quiet* had been translated into 29 languages, and the unknown journalist had been transformed into a world-famous author.

Despite its popularity, the book generated a storm of controversy. Some people charged that Remarque had written solely to shock and to sell. Others called the book sentimental pacifism. The Nazis chose to read it as an attack on the greatness of the German nation. Ignoring the book as literature, they spread rumors to undermine Remarque's popularity. They variously claimed that he was a French Jew, an old man who had never seen a battlefield, or the worthless son of millionaire parents. Remarque refused to comment, later telling an interviewer, "I was only misunderstood where people went out of their way to misunderstand me."

During the controversy Remarque and his wife lived in Berlin. They were divorced in the early 1930s after the Nazis exiled him but remarried almost immediately so that Ilse, who suffered from tuberculosis, would not lose her Swiss residence permit. They lived separately until their final divorce in 1951.

Remarque's sequel to *All Quiet*, based on his and his friends' experiences after they returned from the front, was published in 1931. It was called *Der Weg zurück*, or *The Road Back*. At the time, Remarque was neutral (or noncommittal) rather than a convinced anti-Nazi, but the sequel aroused further Nazi persecution. Goebbels, chief organizer of the witch-hunt, had first brought things to a head in 1930, when the American film version of *All Quiet* was screened in Berlin. His bands of Hitler Youth had rampaged through the theater hurling stink bombs, scattering white mice, and shouting, "Germany, awake!" The film was banned, and in 1931 Remarque was forced to leave Germany, where both his novels were thrown into the fire during the infamous bookburning of 1933.

Remarque commented in 1962, "I had to leave Germany because my life was threatened. I was neither a Jew nor orientated towards the left politically. I was the same then as I am today: a militant pacifist." It is said that Goebbels later invited Remarque back, but that Remarque replied, "What? Sixty-five million people would like to get away and I'm to go back of my own free will? Not on your life!"

In 1932 German officials seized his Berlin bank account—supposedly for back taxes—but he had transferred most of his money as well as his Impressionist paintings to Switzerland, where he bought a villa at Porto Ronco on Lake Maggiore, gradually filling it with valuable antiques.

By the time Remarque was actually deprived of his German citizenship in 1938, his first three books had already been made into films in America and he was sometimes called the King of Hollywood. Until 1939 he divided his time between Porto Ronco and France; from 1939 to 1942 he rented a bungalow in Hollywood. His female companions included Marlene Dietrich and Greta Garbo; his male friends, Charles Chaplin, Cole Porter, F. Scott Fitzgerald, and Ernest Hemingway. Eventually, he tired of the Hollywood glitter, and in 1942 began to divide his time between New York and Porto Ronco. In 1957 he received critical acclaim as an actor for his role in the film version of his novel *A Time to Love and a Time to Die*. In 1958 he married an American actress, Paulette Goddard, whom he had met in the 1940s.

When he first came to America in 1939, Remarque had none of the passport difficulties experienced by most German political exiles at that time. But he felt the injustices of his fellow countrymen deeply and described them fully in his novels. He applied for American citizenship in 1941, becoming a citizen after the time required by law. He loved America—especially the easygoing friendliness of the people—but never felt fully accepted by the Germans and always resented the loss of his German citizenship. Nor was he the only member of his family to suffer at the hands of the Nazis. In 1943 his younger sister Elfriede Scholz was beheaded for spreading subversive propaganda. He was deeply moved when Osnabrück named a street for her in 1968. In 1971 the authorities also named a section of road along the town walls the Erich-Maria-Remarque-Ring.

Wherever he was living he continued to write, and, despite his financial success and love of fine living, never forgot the lessons of World War I. His work eventually included 11 novels, all written in German but immediately translated and published in English as well. They developed themes first introduced in *All*

Quiet. (Each is described in the Further Reading section of this guidebook.) Early in the 1950s Remarque returned briefly to Germany to collect material for a book, but he never returned to his hometown, even when attending his father's funeral near there in 1956. He felt that the new city, rebuilt after World War II, wasn't the town he had enshrined in *All Quiet, The Road Back,* and *The Black Obelisk.*

A series of heart attacks in the late 1960s obliged Remarque to choose Rome instead of New York for his winter quarters, and he lived there and in Porto Ronco until his death in a hospital in Locarno on September 25, 1970.

Tributes from the world press were varied, and sometimes stressed strange things. In his native Germany, the weekly journal *Der Spiegel* published an obituary that managed to omit his ever having written a great World War I novel. Remarque would not have been surprised. The news media had always been far more interested in his glamorous life than in his novels. But the public had bought more than 13 million copies of his books. And *All Quiet on the Western Front,* accounting for 8 million in sales, is still one of the greatest European bestsellers of the 20th century.

THE NOVEL

The Plot

All Quiet on the Western Front tells what happens to a group of German teenagers during World War I. The narrator is Paul Bäumer. He and his classmates had patriotically marched off for recruitment, spurred on by the slogans of their teacher, Kantorek. But they find no glory in war.

As the story opens, 80 men have just returned from two weeks at the front. Seventy of their comrades may be dead or wounded, but their empty bellies concern them more. They nearly riot when the cook won't dish out the food prepared for twice their number. But the commander steps in, and for once they eat their fill. Afterward, Paul and his friends visit their classmate Kemmerich, dying from a leg amputation. All Müller can talk about is who will get Kemmerich's fine leather boots. The more sensitive Kropp laughs bitterly at Kantorek's having called them Iron Youth.

Lounging around the next few days, Paul recalls the basic training methods of the sadistic Corporal Himmelstoss. Cruel as he was, Himmelstoss did a lot more than Kantorek to toughen them for battle. Alone with Kemmerich, Paul can hardly bear it when his friend dies and all the orderly cares about is getting the bed cleared. Outraged at the senseless death of all such frail-looking boys, Paul nevertheless takes Kemmerich's boots to Müller—they are of no use to Kemmerich now.

Soon, underfed replacements arrive. Katczinsky, a scavenger who could find a dinner roast in the Sahara, surprises everyone with beef and beans. He listens as Paul and his friends gleefully recall the night they trapped Himmelstoss with a bedsheet and soundly thrashed him, and joins in as they argue heatedly that the leaders simply ought to slug out their war with each other, while the soldiers watch them.

Horror descends anew the night they string barbed wire at the front. In the dark, the men instinctively avoid incoming shells, but the screaming of horses innocently caught in the bombardment chills them to the bone. When the shelling eases they trudge to a cemetery to wait for transport. Many nearly suffocate in a surprise gas attack, and after a new bombardment their stomachs turn at the sight of dead companions mixed with corpses from blown-up graves. At dawn they mindlessly return to camp.

Resting the next day, Paul's group reluctantly conclude that war has ruined them. After their horrifying experiences, how can they ever again take jobs or studies seriously? Their spirits lift when Himmelstoss appears, sent to the front at last! Tjaden and Kropp openly insult him and leave him sputtering. When the matter is officially reviewed that evening, their light punishment is amply balanced by the lecture Himmelstoss gets on the idiocy of saluting at the front. Much later, Paul and Katczinsky slip off to a farm. Neither squawking goose nor growling bulldog thwarts Paul, and he and his comrade Katczinsky spend a companionable night roasting and eating their goose.

Then it's back to rat-infested trenches at the front. At night they scramble for masks when the enemy sends gas; by day, they cower in stillness to deceive observers in balloons. Terror is their companion through deafening barrages; Paul's dugout survives a direct hit. One night the French infantry attack. All through the next day Paul's company fights in a frenzy, the men armed only with grenades and sharpened shovels. For days, attacks and counterattacks alternate. Once Himmelstoss panics until Paul shouts sense into him and he plunges back into battle. Paul's only relief is to dream of quiet cloisters. By the time the siege ends, only 32 men are left in the company.

Back at a field depot for reorganization, the men loaf and joke as if they hadn't a care in the world. Thinking about their lost comrades would only drive them mad. Even Himmelstoss has changed. Not only did he rescue Westhus, who had been wounded, but, as substitute cook, he is slipping Paul's group badly needed extra rations. Twice, Paul, Kropp, and another classmate, Leer, swim a closely guarded canal, not for the brief pleasures of a soldiers' brothel but for the luxury of hours with three French girls. When Westhus dies after all, Paul—due for leave and temporary reassignment—wonders in agony who will be there when he returns.

On leave in his hometown, Paul relishes the way his classmate Mittelstaedt torments their old schoolmaster Kantorek, now a pitiful specimen of a soldier in the reserve unit Mittelstaedt commands. Nowhere is Paul comfortable. Duty drags him to visit Kemmerich's mother, but his own sensitivity has been dulled by the carnage and he can't begin to comprehend her hysterical grief over a single soldier. His own books and papers no longer comfort him, his civilian clothes don't fit, old men lecture him on how they think the war is really going, and his mother, whom he adores, is seriously ill. So out of place does he feel that he is glad to report for duty at a nearby camp. There he often guards Russian prisoners of war, whom he begins to identify as men like himself and his comrades. The more he sees their suffering, the less he can grasp why he must call them enemy.

When Paul rejoins his company, he is relieved to find that all his closest friends have survived. Polishing is the order of the day; the troops are preparing for an inspection by the Kaiser. The whole ridiculous display leaves them burning with resentment at the blindness of their leaders. Up at the front again, Paul volunteers for a scouting mission with his friends. He is briefly separated from them in the dark trenches and panics until their distant voices steady him. Only comradeship sustains him now. Later, trapped by shelling, he blindly, repeatedly, stabs a French soldier who falls into his foxhole and must listen and watch for hours as the man's life slowly ebbs. He is guilt stricken at having personally killed a plain soldier like himself. It takes the cool way the sniper Oellrich tallies up his kills to snap him back to front-line reality.

By sheer luck Paul's entire group next find themselves guarding an abandoned village and supply dump. For two glorious weeks they lose themselves in feasting, sleeping, and joking. Then, again by chance, both Paul and Kropp receive leg wounds while helping to evacuate a village. During their stay in a Catholic hospital, the wonder of clean sheets soon evaporates, and Paul discovers just how many ways a man can be killed—or maimed for life. The wards seem worse than the battlefield. Kropp's leg is amputated, but Paul recovers.

After a short while Paul is back to animal existence at the front, except that conditions have grown even worse. Starved and short of supplies, the men are emaciated and their nerves so frayed that they are prone to snap at the slightest provocation. It takes only the wonder of cherry blossoms at the edge of a field to madden one man with thoughts of his farm: he deserts and is court martialed. Another, who stoically bore the screaming of the horses in the earlier battle, dies in an insane attempt to rescue a messenger dog.

As the summer of 1918 wears on, existence is reduced to a paralyzing round of filth, mud, disintegrating gear, dysentery, typhus, influenza—and battle. Müller, shot point blank in the stomach, gives Kemmerich's boots to Paul—the boots are sturdy and may survive them all. When pleasure-loving Leer collapses of a hip wound, all Paul has left is his friend Katczinsky. Then even Katczinsky is wounded: his shin is shattered. Paul doggedly carries him far behind the lines to an aid station. But the medics can only shake their heads. Katczinsky has died on Paul's back from a tiny splinter of shrapnel that freakishly pierced his head.

The months wear on to October, and Paul is alone. Back at the front after two weeks of rest for a trace of gas poisoning, he has nothing to hope for. He is killed on a day so quiet that the army report consists of a single line: "All quiet on the Western Front."

The Characters

MAJOR CHARACTERS

Paul Bäumer

Paul Bäumer is the 19-year-old narrator of the story. At the front, Paul's special friends in Second Company include his classmates Behm, Kemmerich,

Müller, Leer, and Kropp. The six of them were among 20 who enlisted together, prodded on by Schoolmaster Kantorek. Although he doesn't say so, Paul is obviously a natural leader: Franz Kemmerich's mother implored him to look after her son when they left home. Paul is also courageous. He may momentarily panic, but he doesn't break under the most terrible battle conditions. He learns the sound of each type of shell; he dives for cover or grabs his gas mask at the right instant. In one battle, he gently comforts an embarrassed rookie who has soiled his underpants, and later soberly contemplates shooting the same man to spare him an agonizing death after his hip has been shattered.

Cool as he is in battle, though, Paul has a hard time making sense of it all. He keeps recalling Behm, the first of his class to die, and when a second—Kemmerich—dies, he rages inwardly at the senseless slaughter of scrawny schoolboys. The callous attitude of commanders and orderlies toward an individual death saddens and disillusions him. His elders were wrong—there is nothing glorious about war—but he has no new values to replace the patriotic myths they taught him.

At first his companions seem shallow to him—immediately forgetting the dead and turning their total attention to stockpiling the cigarets and food originally meant for the deceased soldiers—and he is at pains to tell us why this callousness is necessary. Gradually, though, he comes to accept their approach: that poetry and philosophy and civilian paper-pushing jobs alike, all are utterly pointless in the midst of so much carnage. All you have is the moment at hand, and getting from it all the physical comfort you can is a worthwhile goal. There is another important element, too, to being with your comrades, as going on leave proves to Paul: no civilian understands you the way these men do, and nothing from your former life sustains you the way their friendship does. These values come together for Paul the evening he joins an older friend, Katczinsky, on a goose-hunting raid. They spend the night roasting the goose before eating it, and each time that Paul awakens for his turn at the basting, he feels Katczinsky's presence like a cloak of comfort. At other times, panicked and alone in the dark of the trenches, all it takes to steady his nerves is the sound of his friends' voices. If he awakens from a nightmare, the mere sound of their breathing strengthens him: he is not alone.

Paul gradually comes to realize that the enemy is no different from himself or from one of his friends. The Frenchman he kills in the trenches, Duval, looks like the kind of man whose friendship he would have enjoyed. The Russian prisoners he guards have the same feelings and desires and needs as he. He comes to see war as the ultimate horror. It's bad enough that it pits man against man. But even animals and trees and flowers and butterflies are innocently caught up in the carnage inflicted by Man, the great Destroyer.

As his friends are killed one by one, Paul can only cling to his newfound beliefs in the brotherhood of all men and the value of the spark of life within each individual. At the end, alone, he has only the blind hope that his own mysterious inner spark will somehow survive and guide him after the war. Otherwise, he sees no meaningful future.

Kantorek

Kantorek is a provincial schoolmaster, an energetic little man with a face like a shrew. His whole life centers on the Prussian myth of Destiny: he believes with all his heart that war will bring his country greatness. He sees Paul and his schoolmates not as growing boys but as Iron Youth whose finest destiny lies in serving their Fatherland. His romantic notions change only when he is called up as a reservist and placed under the command of a former pupil named Mittelstaedt. He is a poor excuse of a soldier who shrinks emotionally when Mittelstaedt taunts him with his own former slogans. But even then, we never quite know him as a real human being. He is instead a pathetic illustration of all those elders whose values the young soldier comes to reject.

Corporal Himmelstoss

For most of the novel Himmelstoss is the stereotypical military man who becomes a tyrant in his own small sphere on the basis of a little rank. He sports a waxed mustache and is, like Kantorek, physically undersized. A mail carrier in civilian life, he lets power go to his head. As the corporal in charge of basic training for recruits, he becomes a sadistic drillmaster known as the Terror of Klosterberg. He takes a special dislike to Paul and his friends, being sensitive enough to detect their quiet defiance, and earns the beating they give him one night after trapping him in a bedsheet. Later Himmelstoss is himself assigned to the front, to Paul's company. Before his first battle, he is the same pompous strutter as always, but during the siege he falls into momentary shell shock. Paul snaps him out of it and Himmelstoss fights bravely, together with his former recruits, even rescuing a friend of

Paul. He emerges from battle so changed that he uses his influence to slip Paul's group extra rations.

Stanislaus Katczinsky

Katczinsky, known at Kat, is a 40-year-old, down-to-earth soldier with bent shoulders, blue eyes, and a scraggly mustache. In civilian life he was a cobbler or shoemaker, but he knew a little about all trades. In war he becomes the leader of Paul's group, a welcome substitute for all those older men whose twisted values brought on the war. Despite their differences in age and experience, he forms an especially warm friendship with Paul. Sharp, tough, and resourceful, Kat is unequaled at finding excellent food in the most unlikely places. He is shrewd and cunning—the embodiment of the practical man who can turn his inventive imagination to use in any situation. In the summer of 1918, when Paul is carrying Kat to an aid station for treatment of a shin wound, they recall how Kat once similarly rescued Paul. They reach the station but Kat is dead—killed on Paul's back by a stray splinter to his head. This loss of the last of his friends drains Paul of his one remaining source of comfort at the front.

Franz Kemmerich

The second of Paul's classmates to be killed, Kemmerich dies in great pain after a leg amputation. He had been excellent at gymnastics, but even after a year at the front he is still a slender boy. His nearness to death makes his face look childlike again. His dreams of a simple, peaceful life of forestry work die with him, and Paul trembles with rage at the wastefulness of war. All supplies being scarce at the front, Kemmerich's well-made leather boots are a prize passed on first to Müller and later to Paul. Since they originally came from a downed English flier, the boots become a tangible symbol both of brotherhood and of death as they move from man to man.

Müller

Another volunteer and classmate of Paul, Müller still dreams of passing school examinations. Even during bombardment he mutters propositions in physics. Müller, with his protruding teeth and booming laugh, is a practical man, coarsened by the war. He eats all that is available in anticipation of lean times and asks for Kemmerich's boots even before the unfortunate soldier realizes he is dying. (Müller is indeed the first to inherit the boots and later gives them to Paul before dying of a stomach wound.) His transforming a comrade's death into a chance for good boots is one of the first shocking instances we see of what war does to men.

Leer

Also a volunteer and one of Paul's classmates, Leer shows an interesting mixture of a keen interest in mathematics and an obsession with women. Bearded and battle-hardened, he appears to be at least 40 years old. He claims the blond as his own when he, Paul, and Kropp visit the three French girls. He collapses of a hip wound in the summer of 1918 and bleeds to death within two minutes. Paul thinks, regretfully, what little use his math is now.

Tjaden

Tjaden is a former locksmith with a sharp, thin appearance and an enormous appetite. He is Paul's age, though not one of his classmates. When we first meet him, he is ready to pick a fight with the cook who does not want to serve 80 men the food prepared for twice as many. Because of a bladder problem, Tjaden was considered lazy by Himmelstoss, who persecuted him in basic training. He is bolder at the front, however. He is a fine enough companion in fighting and joking, but Paul and Leer and Kropp dump him when they visit the French girls.

Detering

Detering is a one-dimensional stereotype of the simple, peace-loving peasant. He constantly dreams of his home, his wife, and his farm, and cares little for philosophy or military doctrine. In the spring of 1918, surrounded by battlefield carnage, he is driven nearly mad by the sight of cherry blossoms. They unlock his memories of growing things and, losing all caution, he deserts. He is caught and court martialed.

Albert Kropp

A classmate, volunteer, and special friend of Paul, Kropp is a small man. Since he is regarded as the best thinker in the class, no one is surprised that he is the first to make lance-corporal. In group discussions he is the one who offers profound solutions and comments. It is Kropp, for instance, who suggests turning war into a public festival, with the generals fighting it out in an arena while the common people sit and watch. It is also Kropp who sums up their youth, their disillusionment, and their lack of training for the future by observing, "The war has ruined us for everything." With Paul he is sent to a Catholic hospital behind the lines because of wounds suffered during the evacuation of a village. Scheduled to receive an artificial limb after a leg amputation, he withdraws into long periods of sober silence.

Haie Westhus

Westhus is a 19-year-old peat digger with hands so huge that in one he can conceal a loaf of bread. He operates as Katczinsky's executive on foraging expeditions, and, on the whole, prefers army life to cutting sod. The army gives him food and a place to sleep, and in peacetime would offer what he considers nice, clean work. He is the one member of Paul's group who plans to reenlist after the war but dies of a back wound after being rescued by Himmelstoss.

MINOR CHARACTERS

Bulcke

The fat First Company cook, he is willing to trundle his pots right up to the front lines for his men. He provides a contrast with Ginger.

Ginger

The red-headed Second Company cook is more concerned with his personal safety and regulations than with feeding the men. His pettiness contrasts with Bulcke's courage and generosity.

Josef Behm

One of Paul's classmates, Behm is a plump, homely volunteer who dies two months before he would have been drafted. Wounded in the eye, he is shot down while blindly attempting to return to safety. His death greatly affects his classmates. Later, Mittelstaedt upbraids Kantorek with the fact that had it not been for his marching the whole class down to enlist, Behm would have had at least two more months to live.

Lieutenant Bertinck

Paul's company commander, Bertinck is a fine officer who came up through the ranks. He bears Himmelstoss's complaint and treats Tjaden and Kropp as fairly as possible. He dies saving his companions from an approaching enemy team using a flamethrower.

Heinrich Bredemeyer

Bredemeyer is a soldier and fellow townsman of Paul who tells Paul's mother about the increasing dangers in the front lines. His tactlessness makes Paul's first leave more miserable than it might otherwise have been.

Frau (Mrs.) Bäumer

Paul's mother is a courageous woman who is dying of cancer. She is the most comforting person Paul finds at home. She alone does not pretend to understand what it is like at the front. Paul is in agony over her illness and is overwhelmed by the love she shows him by preparing his favorite foods and depriving herself in order to buy him fine underwear.

Frau (Mrs.) Kemmerich

Unlike Paul's quiet mother, Franz Kemmerich's mother tends to weep and wail. She had unreasonably expected Paul to watch out for her son, Franz, and blames him for surviving while Franz died. The two mothers show different reactions to the brutality of war.

Mittelstaedt

This classmate of Paul takes revenge on schoolmaster Kantorek when the latter is assigned to the home guard unit Mittelstaedt commands. Once Kantorek had held Mittelstaedt's future in his hands by his potential influence in connection with examinations. Aware now that survival is more important than any test, Mittelstaedt ridicules Kantorek, even using the schoolmaster's favorite phrases.

Boettcher

The former porter at Paul's school becomes a model reserve soldier. Mittelstaedt sends him on errands through town with the former schoolmaster, Kantorek, who is an impossible soldier, so that everyone may enjoy the irony of the reversal of roles: the nobody is now the teacher.

Gerard Duval

Duval is a French printer with a wife and child. The soldier Paul instinctively stabs after he falls into Paul's shell hole. Paul's horror grows as he waits hours for Duval to die, and then learns the facts of his life from his wallet. Duval is a pleasant-looking man, and now he is dead at Paul's own hand. Guilt nearly drives Paul mad before a slowdown in the firing finally allows him to leave the shell hole.

Sergeant Oellrich

In contrast to Paul, Oellrich is a sniper who is proud of his ability to pick off enemy soldiers. Katczinsky and Kropp point him out to Paul to shock him back to the reality of front-line warfare after Paul has killed Duval. Oellrich boasts about how his human targets jump when he hits them, and Katczinsky and Kropp remind Paul that the man will probably get a decoration or promotion if he keeps shooting so well.

Josef Hamacher

Hamacher is a popular soldier in Paul and Kropp's hospital ward. He can get away with anything because of a "shooting license," a paper stating that he experiences periods of mental derangement.

Little Peter

Another patient, Peter is small and has black, curly hair. His lung injury is so serious that he is sent to the Dying Room, a room located next to the elevator to the morgue. He vows to return—and does, to everyone's amazement.

Sister Libertine

Sister Libertine is one of the nurses at the hospital where Paul and Albert are patients. Unlike some of the callous medics and surgeons, and even the other serious-minded nuns, she spreads good cheer throughout her entire wing of the hospital. The men would do anything for her.

Franz Wächter

Wächter dies in the hospital. Unable to get anyone to take care of his hemorrhaging arm wound, he makes Paul realize that patients can die just from neglect.

The Three French Girls

Three girls live in a house across the river from a German camp. Paul, Kropp, and Leer swim a closely guarded canal to spend two evenings with them. Leer's favorite is the blond; Paul's girl is the little brunet. She is not particularly concerned that he is going on leave. Considering the shortages, she will welcome any decent soldier, whatever his uniform, if he can also bring food.

Berger

Berger is the strongest soldier in Paul's company. At one time he stoically listened while the screaming horses died, but by the end of the war his protective shell has grown as thin as anyone else's. He loses all judgment and insanely tries to rescue a wounded messenger dog two hundred yards off. He dies of a pelvis wound in the attempt.

Kaiser Wilhelm

William II (1859–1941), or Kaiser Wilhelm, who briefly appears to inspect troops, is a figure from world history. Emperor of Germany and King of Prussia from 1888 to 1918, he was the son of Frederick III and a grandson of both William I of Germany and Queen Victoria of England. When he was a young man, his parents rejected his belief in the divine right of kingship and disliked his impulsiveness and love of military display. These traits have often been explained as his attempts to compensate for a withered left arm. His visit to the troops in this novel shows both his love of military display and his lack of an imposing physical appearance.

His goal was to make Germany a major world power, and he was the dominant force in his own government. He loved foreign travel but often spoke impulsively and insulted other heads of state. His actions helped drive Great Britain into an alliance with France. He engaged in the famous "Willy-Nicky" correspondence with Czar Nicholas of Russia, but undermined the friendship by supporting Austria in policies offensive to Russia. He strained relationships with France by interfering in colonial affairs in Morocco. Alarmed at the growing isolation of Germany, he allied his country with Austria, Italy, and Turkey.

His power declined after the outbreak of the First World War. His abdication was one of the peace requirements demanded by the Allies in 1918.

Other Elements

SETTING

The story told in *All Quiet on the Western Front* occurs during the two years just before the Armistice ended World War I in November 1918. In Chapters 1 and 2 we learn that Paul Bäumer, the narrator, and his friend Kat had been together three years—one year longer than the time period covered by the novel.

By 1916 when the story begins, World War I had already been underway for two years. It broke out in August 1914 between the Allies (Britain, France, Russia, Belgium, Serbia, and later the United States) and the Central Powers (Austria-Hungary and Germany). In June 1914 Austrian Archduke Frances Ferdinand and his wife had been assassinated at Sarajevo by a Serbian nationalist, leading to Austria-Hungary's declaration of war on Serbia. German leaders, alarmed at Russian mobilization and eager to establish the Reich as a power on a par with Britain, declared war on both of Germany's neighbors, Russia and France. They also refused to guarantee the neutrality of Belgium. Great Britain, in turn, declared war on Germany in response to the threat to British allies. At the time,

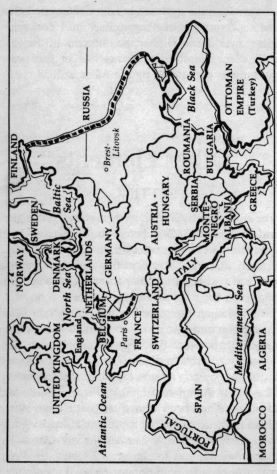

Furthest lines of Central Powers' advance on the Western Front

▬▬▬ Furthest lines of Central Powers' advance on the Eastern Front

Paul and his classmates would have been 16-year-old schoolboys.

German desire to become a major power was nothing new. Prussian beliefs included the idea that Germany had to be a military state because it lacked natural protective boundaries. The Prussian goal was to make Germany a glittering, well-organized, self-confident machine. The idea that Paul rejects—18-year-olds as Iron Youth—fits perfectly into this Prussian mentality.

From the beginning, World War I was fought in two areas, named for their geographical relationship to Germany. The Eastern Front extended into Russia, and the Western Front extended through Belgium into northern France. Germany hoped to knock out France in six weeks and then turn its full strength against Russia. The Allies, however, soon halted the German army at the Marne River, and the war in the West settled down to four years of trench warfare—the static or at a standstill kind of war described in the discussion of Chapter 6 in this guidebook.

In *All Quiet*, Paul describes a battle with the French in Chapter 6 and then, a short time later, is assigned to a camp (Chapter 8) where he guards Russian prisoners of war. Although he does not name the exact locations for the military offensives he describes—after all, the place names had little to do with life and death—the offensive in Chapter 6 could have been the French attack in 1917 at Aisne and Champagne. That offensive failed, with heavy French losses.

Meanwhile, behind the Fronts, all resources were being directed toward winning the war. At first, military methods used were mostly those from earlier wars—infantry, cavalry, and artillery—but this war boosted production of tanks, planes, machine guns, high-explosive shells, flamethrowers, and poison gas.

The strong industrial push left little for civil life, and economies and governments were shattered all over Europe. Forced drafts of men, food shortages, attacks on civilian populations, and hysteria reached heights never before seen.

It is during this final period that the last few chapters of *All Quiet* occur.

By late 1917 Germany had won the war in the East. In March 1918, Russia signed the harsh treaty of Brest-Litovsk, giving Germany huge chunks of its territory. Russia's withdrawal enabled Germany to transfer forces from the East and to mount a supreme effort to capture Paris. But by this time the United States was entering the war, and timing was essential to the German plan: the offensive had to succeed before American troops could reach the Western Front in sizable numbers. Ludendorff, the German leader who directed the operation, was prepared to lose one million men to win. He poured his efforts onto the British sector. The situation became so desperate that the Allies stopped arguing among themselves and established a unified command under Marshal Ferdinand Foch. Nevertheless, at its height the German offensive came within 40 miles of Paris. Then in May 1918 American divisions poured in, and the Allies fought back furiously. In July they broke through the new German lines and swept the Central Powers back toward the pre-1914 frontiers.

In the fall of 1918, German allies began to surrender—in September the Bulgarians, in October the Turks. One by one, ethnic minorities within Austria-Hungary began to proclaim independence, and on November 3 the Austrians capitulated. Germans were demoralized, and mutinies broke out in German fleets. There were revolts among civilians in Kiel and Hamburg. In early November the German king or emperor, Kaiser Wilhelm, fled to Holland. Finally, on November 11, 1918, a German delegation appeared at Allied headquarters to request an armistice.

Overall, the war was fought at tremendous cost. Most tragic was the loss in lives. *Known* dead included 1.8 million German soldiers and more than one million men each from Russia, France, Austria-Hungary, the United Kingdom, and Italy. Even the U.S., latecomer to the war, lost more than 100,000 men. Actual fatalities have been estimated as high as 13 million. In addition, nearly 22 million men were wounded, 7 million of them permanently disabled or mutilated. More than 9 million civilians were also killed.

The world of 1919 was stunned and uncertain. Ten years later the mood still lingered. People wanted to understand what had happened but could not. It is in that atmosphere that Remarque's *All Quiet on the Western Front* appeared.

THEME

In the short note that comes just before Chapter 1, Remarque lets us know exactly what theme he intends. He says that *All Quiet on the Western Front* is the story of a generation of young men who were destroyed by World War I—even if they survived the shelling. To arrive at a full statement of this main theme, Remarque weaves several related themes into the story. The outline that follows points out chapters you can read to see how he presents each idea.

1. THE HORROR OF WAR

Remarque includes discussions among Paul's group, and Paul's own thoughts while he observes Russian prisoners of war (Chapters 3, 8, 9) to show that no ordinary people benefit from a war. No matter what side a man is on, he is killing other men just like himself, people with whom he might even be friends at another time.

But Remarque doesn't just tell us war is horrible. He also shows us that war is terrible beyond anything we could imagine. All our senses are assaulted: we see newly dead soldiers and long-dead corpses tossed up together in a cemetery (Chapter 4); we hear the unearthly screaming of the wounded horses (Chapter 4); we see and smell three layers of bodies, swelling up and belching gases, dumped into a huge shell hole (Chapter 6); and we can almost touch the naked bodies hanging in trees and the limbs lying around the battlefield (Chapter 9).

The crying of the horses is especially terrible. Horses have nothing to do with making war. Their bodies gleam beautifully as they parade along—until the shells strike them. To Paul, their dying cries represent all of nature accusing Man, the great destroyer.

In later chapters Paul no longer mentions nature as an accuser but seems to suggest that nature is simply there—rolling steadily on through the seasons, paying no attention to the desperate cruelties of men to each other. This, too, shows the horror of war, that it is completely unnatural and has no place in the larger scheme of things.

2.   A REJECTION OF TRADITIONAL VALUES

In his introductory note Remarque said that his novel was not an accusation. But we have seen that it is, in many places, exactly that. This accusation—or rejection of traditional militaristic values of Western civilization—is impressed on the reader through the young soldiers, represented by Paul and his friends, who see military attitudes as stupid and who accuse their elders of betraying them.

In an early chapter Paul admits that endless drilling and sheer harrassment did help toughen his group and turn them into soldiers. But he points out, often, how stupid it is to stick to regulations at the front—how insane this basic military attitude becomes in life-and-death situations. One such scene occurs in Chapter 1 when Ginger, the cook, doesn't want to let 80 men eat the food prepared for 150, no matter how hungry they are. Another occurs in Chapter 7 when Paul is walking around in his hometown and a major forces him to march double time and salute properly—a ridiculous display, considering what he has just been through at the front. The emptiness of all this spit and polish shows up again in Chapter 9 when the men have to return the new clothes they were issued for the Kaiser's inspection: rags are what's real at the front.

The betrayal of the young by their elders becomes an issue on several occasions. In the first two chapters of the book we learn how misguided Paul was by the teachings of parents and schoolmasters. We also see how older people cling to the Prussian myth of the glory of military might when Paul goes home on leave in Chapter 7. The Kaiser's visit in Chapter 9 adds some hints of Remarque's specific disillusionment with the leaders of his own country. From a broad study of literature and world history, we can see that these older people were not individually to blame for their views. They were simply handing on what was handed on to them. Still, we can also understand why Paul and his friends are so bitterly disappointed and so angry to discover that their elders were wrong. Most readers feel a little sad that young men should consider the act of ridiculing adults their greatest goal in life, but we can also understand why they take revenge on Himmelstoss and Kantorek (Chapters 3 and 7). We even get a certain kick out of what they do, understanding their need to take out their disappointment on someone they know. These situations are, in miniature, an acting out of the bitter anger and disillusionment Paul feels when he says in Chapter 10, "It must all be lies and of no account when the culture of a thousand years could not prevent this stream of blood being poured out."

3. FRIENDSHIP: THE ONLY ENDURING VALUE

The theme of comradeship occurs often and gives the novel both lighthearted and sad moments. In Chapter 5 it's easy to overlook how the farmer felt about having his property stolen and to chuckle aloud when Paul is struggling to capture the goose! We appreciate the circle of warmth that encloses him and Kat that night as they slowly cook and eat the goose, and then extend their warm circle by sharing the leftovers with Kropp and Tjaden. In Chapter 10 we enjoy their sharing of the pancakes and roast pig and fine club chairs at the supply dump, and we understand why Paul fakes a high temperature to go to the same hospital as Albert Kropp.

Friendship emerges as an even more important theme at the front. In Chapters 10 and 11 we see men helping wounded comrades at great personal risk— or even, like Lieutenant Bertinck, dying for their friends. The handing on of Kemmerich's fine yellow leather boots also acts as a symbol of friendship—a symbol we can almost touch, and one that keeps us aware of how deeply a soldier feels the loss of each of his special friends. We can understand how hearing the voices of friends when one is lost (Chapter 9) or even just hearing their breathing during the night

(Chapter 11) can keep a soldier going. We grieve with Paul and almost put down the book when Kat dies.

4. A GENERATION DESTROYED BY WORLD WAR I

Taking all of the themes together and adding Paul and his friends' hopeless discussions of what is left for them to do after the war (Chapter 5), we can conclude that Remarque succeeds in his main theme: showing that Paul's generation was destroyed by the Great War, as World War I was then called.

STYLE AND STRUCTURE

All Quiet on the Western Front is, on the whole, a very serious and even a grim novel. Remarque presents his message through vivid description and imagery. The tone is not overwhelmingly bitter.

Two things stand out in Remarque's style: his vivid word pictures and the way he balances contrasting scenes against each other to make each one stand out.

His descriptions bring every chapter to life, whether he is showing us the glare of flares or the darkness beyond the trenches, vicious rats or itchy lice, the steady drumlike beat of bombardment or the piercing shrieks of shells and wounded. His descriptions also include images of beauty and peace—usually in Paul's thoughts—that make clear how awful the front actually is. He converts a pair of boots, a goose, and the circle of light cast by campfires into symbols of friendship. And he uses similes to show the brutality of war: the men fight *like* thugs, *like* wild beasts. The tanks push relentlessly forward *like* steel beasts squashing bugs.

Ch.	Far from the Front	Near the Front	At the Front
1	Recollections: school, Kantorek.	Second Company, down to 80 men, well fed.	
2	Recollections: Himmelstoss, basic training.	Kemmerich's death in a field hospital. The boots.	
3	Reminiscences: Himmelstoss.	Kat's skill at foraging. Theories of war.	
4			Barbed wire duty. The wounded horses. The upturned graves.
5		Insubordination to Himmelstoss. Lack of post-war goals. The goose incident.	
6			Days upon days of trench warfare. Company down to 32 men. Westhus wounded.

Ch.	*Far from the Front*	*Near the Front*	*At the Front*
7	Paul home on leave. Mittel-staedt's humilia-tion by Kantorek.	The evening with the French girls.	
8	Paul guarding the Russian prisoners of war.		
9		The Kaiser's visit.	Paul's killing of Duval in the trench.
10	The hospital. Kropp left behind.	The supply dump.	
11			Starvation, lack of supplies, demoral-ization. Loss of Detering, Müller, Leer, Kat.
12			Paul's death on a quiet day.

Remarque's use of contrast, gives a new meaning to the phrase "theater of war." He keeps us moving between the trenches and the rest of the world. Even if Paul's hometown is suffering from war shortages, life there is safe and comfortable compared with the front. Even the hospital, filled with wounded, offers clean sheets and regular food—luxuries unimaginable at the front lines. These contrasts help us to understand what is happening to the emotional life of the young soldier.

The following chart will help you see more clearly how Remarque uses contrasts. The first part of *All Quiet* dwells on what happened at home, far from the front, and what it is like near the front. The middle chapters actually take us to the front and then pull us back several times—to civilian life, to a camp behind the lines, to a supply dump, to a hospital—so that we too feel the shock when we return, in the final chapters, to the unrelieved pressures of the front.

Finally, Remarque's style includes irony. We fully appreciate how little value is attached to a single human life by 1918 when we read the army report on the progress of the war on the day Paul dies: "All quiet on the Western Front."

POINT OF VIEW

Stories usually are told from the first person or the third person point of view. We get these terms from grammar. "I love" is a first person structure, "you love" is second person, and "he (or she) loves" is third person. A story is told in the first person when the narrator says that *I* or *we* are doing thus-and-so: someone actually in the story is telling it. A third person story uses the *he* or *they* approach; some unnamed person outside the story is observing others doing something.

Except for the very last two paragraphs of the book, *All Quiet on the Western Front* is written from the first person point of view. The story is being told by someone who is actually in it—Paul Bäumer—not by some invisible outsider. Remarque does switch to third person in the last two paragraphs for an obvious reason: Paul cannot report his own death.

First person narration always has both advantages and disadvantages. A big advantage is that we tend to identify with the main character. In *All Quiet* we feel as if we are right there with Paul, experiencing what he is seeing and hearing and feeling. We almost think his thoughts, share his ideas. First person narration makes the whole story seem direct and real and honest.

On the other hand, first person narration also limits us to knowing and seeing only what the narrator—in this case, Paul—knows and sees. We get other news and views and opinions only as he filters them and reports them to us.

In the case of *All Quiet*, Paul is young and immature. Until he enlisted, he had never experienced real pain or tragedy in his life. Older people generally know from experience that human beings can survive incredible pain and still find meaning in life. Paul hasn't had any time to gain that kind of experience to sustain him. Therefore it's asking quite a bit to have us accept, from him, whole theories about war and life and the nature of human beings. Still, whatever Paul might lack in age or experience is balanced for us by the honesty and sensitivity we see in him.

Over all, then, in *All Quiet on the Western Front*, the advantages of first person narration outweigh the disadvantages. There is a perfect fit of first person point of view with what Remarque wanted to say about World War I—that it destroyed a whole generation of the young. How better to show us that than to let us experience the war through the eyes of a young soldier?

FORM

When critics use the word form to discuss a novel, they sometimes mean its overall style and structure—the elements already presented under that heading in this guidebook. Another meaning of form is the category a novel falls into—how it should be classified, what kind of fiction it is.

You yourself use form in this narrow, second meaning when you say that you like to read mysteries or westerns or romances or some other kind of story. But if someone asked you what kind of book *All Quiet* is, you would find that it just doesn't fit standard classifications. You might say it's a war story—but it's a lot more than that. It's also a story about a boy turning into a disillusioned adult, or perhaps a story telling society that it ought to eliminate the great evil of war. The standard categories simply do not express all that.

The best term for a novel in which everything depends on a specific war setting is historical novel. Charles Dickens' *A Tale of Two Cities*, set during the French Revolution, is an example. *All Quiet* does happen during World War I, but Remarque doesn't dwell on historical details such as names of battles. Instead he concentrates much more on what any war does to people.

Usually a novel in which a young person matures by passing through some kind of crisis is called a novel of formation or a novel of initiation. This fits Stephen Crane's *The Red Badge of Courage*, in which Henry Fleming starts out as a naive boy, expecting war to be glorious, only to find how terrible it is. It also fits

All Quiet to some extent, but not as well—by the time the book begins, Paul has already become disillusioned enough to call 70 deaths a "miscalculation."

If you see *All Quiet* as a novel telling society something wrong ought to be changed—in this case, war—you could try sociological novel, but again the label seems somehow off. It fits a book against slavery like Harriet Beecher Stowe's *Uncle Tom's Cabin* but seems to express only one element of *All Quiet*.

All in all, form as classification is simply too narrow and artificial for this book. With *All Quiet*, you are better off using the word form in its broad senses meaning style and structure. *All Quiet* can be described as a novel made up of dramatic scenes, vivid language, and a series of contrasting episodes that make us feel how totally destructive war is.

The Story

AUTHOR'S NOTE

Remarque begins his book with a note before the first chapter. In it he says that his book "is to be neither an accusation nor a confession, and least of all an adventure," but rather an account of a generation of young men who were destroyed by the war—World War I—"even though they may have escaped its shells."

What does he mean? Biography and history tell us his situation. By 1929 when his book came out, World War I had been over for ten years, but it was still affecting people like him and his friends, who had gone from the schoolroom right into the trenches.

Many of them survived, but they felt as if a shadow still hung over their lives. After all that time, they still hadn't been able to sort out their feelings about the war.

Remarque says that he doesn't want to accuse or blame anyone, that he certainly doesn't have anything new to confess, and that he is definitely not trying to write an adventure story—the kind of war story that's full of heroes and waving flags.

If all of that is what we should not expect, then what should we expect? Well, if he means what he says, he's going to let the story itself show us just exactly what was so destructive about World War I. Maybe it's the deaths of friends; maybe it's the loss of ideals. We'll need to read the book to find out. But we can expect every chapter to tell us something to support his theme: that the First World War destroyed even those who came through it alive.

CHAPTER 1

The very first paragraph takes us within five miles of the front lines. The men are resting on the ground, having just stuffed themselves with beef and beans (the cook is still dishing out more). There are double rations of bread and sausage besides, and tobacco is so plentiful that everyone can get his preference— cigarets, cigars, or chews. Whoever is telling the story is right there, in it; this is what is called first person narration. But the narrator (we soon find out that he's 19 years old and his name is Paul Bäumer) makes clear that the whole situation is incredible:—"We have not had such luck as this for a long time."

Where did the windfall come from? Paul says, "We have only a miscalculation to thank for it." It turns out that the quartermaster sent, and the cook prepared, food for the full Second Company—150 men. But 70 were killed at the end of a quiet two-week mission when the English suddenly opened up with high-explosive field guns.

Before we can stop to think about Paul's dismissing all those deaths as a miscalculation, he backs up to tell the whole story of how they nearly had to riot to get all that food and tobacco. The cook, it seems, didn't care about the count; he just didn't want to give any man more than a single share. In the course of retelling how their noise brought the company commander, who finally ordered the cook to serve everything, Paul introduces all his friends.

They're an assorted lot: first, three of his classmates from school—Müller, the bookworm, Albert Kropp, the sharp thinker, and bearded Leer who likes officers' brothels. Then there are three other 19-year-olds: the skinny locksmith Tjaden, the farmer Detering, and the peat-digger Haie Westhus. Finally he names an older soldier—the group's shrewd, 40-year-old leader, a man with a remarkable nose for food and soft jobs, Stanislaus Katczinsky.

NOTE: From their names we see that these major characters are German, but it really doesn't matter. They could just as well be French or English, so far as their experiences are concerned.

At this point we don't really know if Paul, the narrator, is as cold and unfeeling as he appears. He and his friends seem to care much more about food than about the lives of their companions. Is Remarque indirectly telling us that war reduces people to animals? Or are the men just being realistic? We'll have to wait and see.

The day continues to be "wonderfully good," says Paul, because their mail catches up with them. But one letter angers them. It's from their schoolmaster, Kantorek, who pumped them all so full of the glory of fighting for their country that they marched down to the district commandant together and enlisted. The only one who had to be persuaded was homely Josef Behm, and he's dead already—the first of their class to fall. Paul doesn't blame Kantorek personally for Behm's death, but he does blame the "thousands of Kantoreks" who were so sure their view of the coming war was the right one. We were only 18, he says; we trusted our teachers and our parents to guide us, and "they let us down so badly." He seems to be saying that the war has cut them adrift from a meaningful life, with no new values to replace the old ones. All the young soldiers know for sure is that it's good to have a full belly or a good smoke.

The friends go over to visit Franz Kemmerich, a classmate who is dying after a leg amputation. Müller turns out to be totally crude and tactless. Kemmerich is dying, and Müller rattles on about Kemmerich's stolen watch and just who will get Kemmerich's fine English leather boots. Paul, on the other hand, recalls Kemmerich's mother, crying and begging Paul to look after Franz as they left for the front. To Paul, Kemmerich still looks like a child accidentally poured into a military uniform. Perhaps war hasn't blunted his sensitivity yet, but Müller's crudeness shocks us.

As they leave the dressing station, it is obvious that Kropp, like Paul, is still brimful of feelings. Erupting into anger, he hurls his cigaret to the ground and mutters, "Damned swine!" He is thinking of the leaders who sent them into battle and of people like Kantorek calling waifs like Kemmerich "Iron Youth." "Youth!" thinks Paul. "That is long ago. We are old folk."

NOTE: The Romantic View of War   From history
we know that the Kantoreks passionately believed the
ideals they taught their children and students. World
War I broke out in what seems to us a largely innocent
world, a world that still associated warfare with glorious cavalry charges and the noble pursuit of heroic
ideals. Everyone—Allies and Central Powers alike—
expected a quick, clean war with a glorious aftermath.
Most Europeans, not just Germans, saw war as the
adventure of a lifetime. The popular English poet
Rupert Brooke thanked God in his poem "1914" for
waking "us from sleeping" and providing the oppor-
tunity to do something new and clean in "a world
grown old and cold and weary." Americans were no
different, though Stephen Crane's Civil War novel *The
Red Badge of Courage*—showing war in all its ugli-
ness—had been around for 20 years. Listen to the
lighthearted tone of patriotic World War I songs by
George M. Cohan. Later in the war and afterwards,
poets and novelists (including Remarque) dispelled
the myth. The English poet Siegfried Sassoon wrote
about a battlefield, "I am staring at a sunlit picture of
hell."

CHAPTER 2

We get to know Paul better in the second chapter. It
is the next day and he is still thinking about his parents and about Kantorek. He recalls school life, hob-
bies, poetry writing, and observes, "of this nothing
remains." The older men have wives and jobs to
return to; the war is just an interruption for them. But
the "Iron Youth" had not yet taken root: "The war
swept us away" and they don't know how it will end.
"We know only that in some strange and melancholy

way we have become a waste land." He goes on to defend Müller's preoccupation with Kemmerich's boots—Müller is just being practical, he says. After all, Kemmerich has no further use for them. Paul claims that Müller would go barefoot over barbed wire rather than plot to get the boots if Kemmerich could use them. But as things are, Müller, who does need them, is much more entitled to them than some thieving hospital orderly.

NOTE: Let's pause a moment. Why is Paul working so hard to excuse Müller? Does he protest so much because there's a bit of Müller in himself? He certainly has an intellectual grasp of the situation and probably wrote good essays in school. Look at the phrases he can produce: "[W]e have become a waste land." Does he secretly wish he could translate his ideas into action as bluntly as Müller?

Another question: Remember how Remarque said in his opening note that his book was not going to be an accusation? Is it or isn't it? An author usually speaks through his main characters—at this point, Paul. Paul says he doesn't blame the Kantoreks. Judging from all you already know of Paul, what do you think? Does he truly know his own feelings? Or do you think some bitterness he doesn't even recognize might underlie his words?

A definite note of bitterness creeps into Paul's next thoughts, but there's a strong trace of nostalgia, too. Now that he has experienced front-line fighting, boot camp, rough as it was, almost seems like the good old days! He recalls how quickly you learned that in the army, all the learning from Plato to Goethe is less important than knowing how to spring to attention or keep your buttons polished. He particularly reviews the cruel treatment he and his friends endured at the hands of the sadistic Corporal Himmelstoss, a former mailman. Under his orders Paul once scrubbed the corporals' dining room with a toothbrush, and another morning he remade the man's bed 14 times! Often the whole group ended drills covered with mud, or stood at attention for long sessions, without gloves, in freezing weather. Every rotten job in the camp came their way, but Himmelstoss never broke them. Eventually, under Kropp's instigation, they developed the tactic of obeying Himmelstoss's orders so slowly that even he gained a certain respect for them and eased up on them a fraction. How insane such training was, Paul thinks, but you can almost see him grin as he adds, how well it worked! It made them hard, suspicious, bitter, and tough—not so great for civillian life, but perfect preparation for the trenches! Such discipline, Paul concludes, was exactly what they needed as recruits.

Paul continues to spend his day quietly. He goes alone to visit Kemmerich and says all the soothing things people say about a bright future when they know very well that someone is dying. But Kemmerich knows. He asks Paul to give his boots to Müller. For an hour Paul watches as his friend cries silently. He cannot get an orderly to help when death sounds begin to gurgle in Kemmerich's throat. Instead the orderly urges him to hurry up and clear out Kemmerich's things; he needs the bed. Really, the orderly has acted no worse than the whole company yesterday, clamoring for the food their dead companions couldn't eat. And the orderly at least wants the bed for another man. But this time it hits Paul. He can't be indifferent or uncaring. He's had time to see what a young boy his friend still is; he's had time to rage at the senseless brutality that sends boys out to be killed for nothing. He gulps and leaves the huts as the orderlies haul Kemmerich onto a waterproof sheet. Paul's feet seem to push him forward and he finds himself feeling a strength rising up from the earth into his body. He is alive and he is glad! "The night lives, I live." He takes the boots to Müller, who immediately tries them on. They fit well.

NOTE: Imagery and Symbolism   As Paul leaves the dressing station, his mind fills with thoughts of *girls, flowery meadows, white clouds*. Watch for the return of such images whenever Paul is overcome by the brutality and senselessness of the carnage—the butchery—of battle.

Keep an eye, too, on *Kemmerich's boots*. He was not the first owner. In Chapter 1 the boots were described as "airman's boots. They are fine English boots of soft, yellow leather which reach to the knee and lace up all the way." It doesn't take too much imagination, considering the state of aviation in 1916, to figure out how Kemmerich got the boots. Assuming the English airman is dead, the boots have now gone to their third owner—and fit him, too. Are all soldiers interchangeable, whatever side they are on? And how many owners will the boots outlast?

CHAPTER 3

Reinforcements arrive. Some are older, but many are even younger than Paul and his schoolmates. When Kropp calls them "infants," Paul agrees. He and Kropp strut around feeling like "stone-age veterans." It's been a few days since the big feast, and everyone is astonished when Katczinsky ("Kat") produces a tub of beef and bean stew. He patiently teaches the new recruits the proper etiquette—payment next time with a cigar or chew of tobacco—but lets his friends off free, "of course." Paul recalls admiringly how Kat can stroll off and find hot bread, horse meat, and even salt and a frying pan in the midst of desolation. His masterpiece was four boxes of lobster, although his friends, admittedly, would rather have had a good steak.

It's a pleasant, drowsy day. Kropp has washed his socks and spreads them out to dry. Kat and Paul lean up against the sunny side of the hut. In the air there's a smell of tar and summer and sweaty feet. The men's rest period is, for us, like a bridge between the results of battle and actual battle. We saw the results in Chapters 1 and 2—more food for some, death for others. But we know of slaughter only by hearsay; Kemmerich died a comparatively clean death. We have yet to experience shelling, gassing, and butchery; they will come in Chapter 4.

This chapter, meanwhile, gives us more background on Paul's classmates and friends, and lets us see and hear infantry soldiers at rest. What kinds of things do such men talk about? What do you think you would talk about in their situation?

Kat wants to talk about saluting. Tjaden failed to salute a major, so they've all been practicing, and Kat can't get it out of his head. He maintains their side is losing the war because they salute too well. Kropp, the thinker, begins to argue with him. Meanwhile they bet a bottle of beer on the outcome of an airfight going on far above them. For the attention they pay, you would think those were toy planes battling up there, but the man who will die is flesh and blood.

Kropp and Kat begin to argue about the management of war. Kat wants to drop all the saluting and military drill and adopt the principle in a piece of verse he knows: If everyone got the same grub and pay, "the war would be over and done in a day." The more philosophical Kropp, riled up as always about injustice, argues that war ought to be run like a festival, with such things as tickets and bands. The main event would be the generals and ministers of the two countries, dressed in swimsuits and armed with clubs, slugging it out in an arena. The winning side would be the one whose leaders survived. To Kropp that sounds a whole lot more fair than the situation they're in, where the wrong people do the fighting. (Maybe Remarque didn't intend his book to be an accusation, but it gets harder and harder to say that it does not indict the blindness of early 20th-century world leaders.)

The heat reminds Paul of the training camp barracks, with heat shimmering over the square. In hindsight the cool rooms seem inviting.

Meanwhile the German plane above them has been shot down and plummets headlong in streamers of smoke. It is Kropp who bet on that plane. Talk turns to reminiscences of Corporal Himmelstoss and basic training. Earlier, Paul had observed that little men cause much of the pain in this world. They are so much more energetic and uncompromising than the big fellows. Kantorek was small, and so is Himmelstoss. Kat observes that power always corrupts officers, especially those who were insignificant (little?) in civilian life. Kropp suggests that discipline really is necessary, but Kat shoots back that the kind of discipline taught in boot camp is practically criminal. Boys learn to drill and salute, and then think they know how to survive at the front!

At this point Tjaden, his face red with excitement, rushes up with news—Himmelstoss is joining their unit! Tjaden has special reason to hate the man: Himmelstoss put him and another bedwetter in the same set of bunks so they would disgust and "cure" each other. Since neither could help himself, one always ended up sleeping on the cold floor. Meanwhile Haie Westhus, the peat-digger, ambles over, sits down, and winks at Paul. Paul recalls how Tjaden, Westhus, Kropp, and he himself "squared accounts" with Himmelstoss the night before they left for the front. They ambushed him with a bedsheet as he left his favorite pub and gleefully—though anonymously—gave him a royal beating. Himmelstoss ought to have been pleased, Paul comments ironically, at how well the "young heroes" had learned his cruel methods!

NOTE: Air Power   Balloons were used for reconnaissance and observation by French forces in Italy in 1859 and by Union forces during the American Civil War. Paul later mentions their use in World War I as well. By 1914, successful models had demonstrated the feasibility of motor-driven airplanes, but it was the war itself that provided motivation for research and development of aircraft. At the beginning of the war Germany established its superiority in the air. The Fokker monoplane, with a fixed machine gun that could fire forward through the propeller blades, inspired Allied efforts. Developments and counterdevelopments followed, pushing the Allies ahead, and led to formation flying, aerial dogfights, and aerial bombing of enemy lines of communication and ammunition depots. Later in the novel—toward the end of the war—Paul mentions flyers making a game of pursuing individual soldiers. Still, during World War I, planes were employed mostly in support of ground forces. Development of air forces as a separate military branch followed World War I as the military capabilities of aircraft became more evident.

CHAPTER 4

One night the men are trucked to the front to ram in iron stakes and to string barbed wire. It's a warm evening, a pleasant drive, and the men smoke as they roll along. They're not concerned about lurching into potholes the driver can't see without headlights. Many a man would just as soon he pitched out and sent home with a broken arm earned that way! Kat and Paul distinctly hear geese as they pass one house. They exchange glances—another Katczinsky raid is due when they return! At the front, they find the air acrid, with guns reverberating and shells whistling and exploding. The English have started early. Kat senses a bombardment coming, and at the front his opinion is gospel. Paul already feels as if he's entered a whirlpool which is sucking him into its spinning depths. Only clinging to the ground helps; the earth is like a mother offering shelter.

NOTE: Apostrophe to Earth   In the paragraph following "Earth!—Earth!—Earth!," Paul prays directly to the earth. The name of this poetic device or rhetorical figure of speech is apostrophe. It is an address to an absent, abstract, or inanimate being. When that being is a god, the technique is called invocation. Read the paragraph carefully. Could it be considered an invocation? If so, what additional weight does this lend to Paul's thought in the preceding paragraph, "To no man does the earth mean so much as to the soldier"?

The men become alert animals, throwing themselves to the ground instinctively just before a storm of fragments flies overhead. It is not conscious, but without obeying this animal insight, no soldier would survive. Columns of men move past into the mist like a dark wedge. Gleaming horses pass with the ammunition wagons, their riders looking like knights of another age. Paul and his group load up with iron stakes and rolls of barbed wire, and they stumble all the way to the front line in the dark. Bombardment lights the sky. Amid the sounds of the bombardment, Paul and his group string barbed wire.

NOTE: Onomatopoeia   The technique in which the sound of a word imitates its meaning is called onomatopoeia, as in the word hiss. Find other onomatopoetic words in Paul's description of the sounds of bombardment, both in this paragraph and in paragraphs later in the chapter. What effect do these words have on your awareness of what it must have been like at the front? If you were filming this novel, how would you create these sounds?

Finally, after hours of work, the job is done: the barbed wire has been strung. Paul's hands are torn from handling the close-set spikes, and the night has turned cold. Shells are still shrieking and pounding overhead, and beams of light sweep through the overhead mist. One searchlight pins an airman like a bug, and he is shot down. The scene assaulting our eyes and ears is terrifying—a misty, steaming, roaring hell—but what happens to Paul? He falls sound asleep! Our picture of Paul fills out: he is that experienced, old soldier he claims to be, knowing when he is in danger and when he is not. Still, he awakens confused. Momentarily, he mistakes the glare of rockets for gala fireworks at a party. He doesn't know where he is or whether it's day or night; he feels like a lost child. But Katczinsky is sitting protectively near, calmly smoking a pipe. He tells Paul it's all right; it was just a shell landing nearby that startled him. He sounds for all the world like a daddy comforting a child who's had a nightmare. Paul, in turn, acts like a kindly father when a frightened recruit creeps right into his arms. The blond boy hides his head, and his thin little shoulders remind Paul of Kemmerich. Paul gently moves the youngster's fallen helmet to his buttocks where it will protect him best. Moments later a new bombardment so terrifies the boy that he empties his bowels, and he blushes with shame. But Paul offers no ridicule—he just sends him behind a bush to throw away his underpants.

The bombardment eases, but terrible cries break out—the screaming of horses. Detering, a farmer, finds their agony unendurable and cries for someone to shoot them. He even aims his own gun, though they're much too far away, and Kat has to knock his rifle into the air lest he hit a man. The appalling sounds continue, and some of the wounded horses run berserk, dragging their own intestines. The men in Paul's area hold their hands over their ears; they can't bear it, yet there's absolutely nothing they can do. Finally the horses are shot and it is mercifully still.

NOTE: The Horses   If you think back to Paul's earlier comments on the horses, you can see how deeply he appreciates the beauty of nature. Now he identifies their pain as nature itself protesting the savagery of human beings. To him the cries of the horses are "the moaning of the world, . . . martyred creation, wild with anguish." It would not have been Paul alone who saw the horses as symbolic of all of creation. We tend to use the words romance and romantic to mean love story. But in literature, romantic means an 18th- and 19th-century emphasis on mysticism, feeling, and sympathy for nature. That's the kind of literature Paul and his companions would have been familiar with before they were plunged into the war.

The presence of the horses also helps set the time of this novel. Horses and donkeys were used extensively in the First World War, since trucks, tanks, and planes were still in the early stages of development. That's also why Paul calls trucks motor lorries, to distinguish them from horse-drawn wagons, which were still sometimes called, in English, trucks or lorries.

As readers, we almost sigh with relief when the troops trudge back at three in the morning toward the place where the trucks will pick them up. They make their way through trenches and a small forest, and into a cemetery, but Kat, whose feelings are always accurate at the front, is uneasy. He's right: another bombardment begins. This time Paul receives a blow on the head and is struck by flying splinters, but he is not seriously wounded. Ironically, it is a coffin that shelters him; the arm he feels is that of a long-dead corpse, not a fellow soldier.

Bells and metal clappers warn of a new danger, poison gas. Paul and Kat don their gas masks in time, but some of the new recruits do not. They will cough out their seared lungs in clots. History tells us that gas victims died in great pain, their faces burnt and blackened. Tensely waiting to see if their masks are functioning, Kat and Paul and Kropp scowl at the obscene stuff, the gas hanging like a jellyfish over the field. A new bombardment churns up the cemetery, as if killing the dead a second time. When the explosions ease, Paul and Kat—heads buzzing from the stale air circulating through their masks—dig a man out from under a coffin, dumping the corpse to make the work go better. They bandage their comrade, using a coffin board. They also bandage the rookie that Paul comforted earlier. His hip is shattered and they think of shooting him as an act of kindness, but too many men gather. War may be war, but it's still not right to shoot a man in cold blood. Two dead men lie in an upturned grave; the living throw more dirt over them. The earth may sometimes protect a man, but as Paul will comment later on, she also erases all sign of his ever having existed.

NOTE: The Indifference of Nature   Earlier in this chapter Paul thought of the screaming of the horses as nature crying out in protest at what man was doing. If you keep an eye out for other comments on nature as the story develops, you'll notice that he never does this again. Instead, his references to nature show that earth simply covers the dead and erases their identities. It's like the poem "Grass" by American poet Carl Sandburg. Nature just doesn't care one way or another, but goes calmly on. Grass covers all signs of what happened on a battlefield just as easily as it covers a front lawn. In Chapter 11 we will also see how the seasons march on, paying no attention at all to the desperate gyrations of the two-legged beings struggling on the surface of the earth. Blossoms come out in spring; rain during the summer leaves the men soaked and caked with mud. Nature is so big it doesn't even notice man.

At last Paul's unit clambers numbly into the trucks, too battered to care about the insensitive men at the dressing station with all their babbling about numbers and labels. Driving back to camp, the standing men mindlessly duck their heads at each call of "Wire"—a warning of low, dense, overhead telephone lines. It is raining, and the rain, Paul says, "falls in our hearts."

CHAPTER 5

After the nightmare in Chapter 4, we're ready for some relief, and this chapter offers it. Remarque—or Paul—shows us by contrast how friendship can create a tiny island within the sea of death.

Once again the men idle behind the lines, nonchalantly killing lice while they talk about plans for after the war. Suddenly the newly assigned Himmelstoss appears and roles are reversed: they are the veterans. Tjaden sneers at the man and rudely refuses to salute. The others enjoy the encounter, but, once it is over and Tjaden and Himmelstoss have stormed off in different directions, they go right back to their discussion. Paul does some counting—of the twelve privates among the 20 classmates who volunteered as a group, seven are already dead, four are wounded, and one is insane. Müller and Kropp and Paul feel lost. Kat and Westhus and even Himmelstoss can return to their old jobs after the war, but what future do Müller, Kropp, and Paul have? Kropp, the intellectual, puts the fate of his generation into the simplest of words: "The war has ruined us for everything." Paul agrees. They no longer care about "achieving" or believe in the progress of civilization. They know only war.

The discussion ends when Himmelstoss comes steaming back. He wants Tjaden. Kropp and Müller comment on ways to "get" Himmelstoss, and Paul observes how pitiful their goals have become. The biggest ambition they have left is to knock the conceit out of a mailman. Half an hour later Himmelstoss is back, still seeking Tjaden. He interrupts their card game. Kropp angrily points to puffs of antiaircraft fire high above them and tells Himmelstoss off: What does he want them to do? Salute and ask permission before they die? Himmelstoss disappears like a comet, with Kropp obviously added to his complaint list.

That evening Lieutenant Bertinck gives Himmelstoss's complaints a fair review, and he does punish Kropp and Tjaden but only lightly, with open arrest behind wire fencing instead of closed arrest, locked up in a cellar. Kat and Paul play cards with the two prisoners far into the night, but events haven't erased Kat's memory of the geese. With a little bribery, he and Paul hitch a ride to the spot. And then we enjoy the most comic scene of the novel! Try reading it aloud: Paul, in the goose-shed, battling a bulldog and kicking geese in order to steal a goose and toss it to Kat. Our formerly law-abiding schoolboy is even ready to shoot some farmer's dog to steal the man's property! But to Kat and Paul, it's a soldier's right to supplement his rations however he can. At last Paul succeeds, and he and Kat spend the rest of the night in quiet camaraderie in an out-of-the-way shed, cleaning, roasting, basting, and eating all the goose they want. Near dawn they pack up the feathers for later use. Extending their circle of peace and brotherhood, they take the rest of the meat to Tjaden and Kropp. For the moment, all's right in their world.

CHAPTER 6

This chapter opens a whole new stage in the novel. Battered and numbed as Chapter 4 left Paul and his friends, with its screaming horses and twice-killed corpses, it was only one night—a series of flash impressions of war. Now Remarque moves Paul—

and us—into the deadening cage of weeks of trench warfare. In 1929 a few critics accused Remarque of sensationalizing the war in chapters like this one, of deliberately trying to shock readers to sell more books. The National Socialists, or Nazis, who were then coming to power, pounced on every mention of worn-out equipment or lack of supplies as an attack on the Fatherland. But everyone else found Remarque's account, if anything, an understated report on the horrors of war for men on either side. Things that we would scream about at home—infestations of rats or days without food—are simply reported as facts of the soldier's life. The chapter also helps us see why fighting men sometimes lose religious faith: they see only blind luck in operation on the battlefield, no evidence of the orderly plan of a loving God. For men Paul's age, a scene glimpsed on the way to the front says it all: brand new coffins, stacked against a bombed-out schoolhouse. The scene predicts their future and shows that nothing remains of their past.

NOTE: World War I Trench Warfare   In World War I, attacks changed from those of earlier wars, since a machine gun behind barbed wire could mow down whole columns of attackers. Flag-waving cavalry charges were replaced with prolonged bombardment, followed by days upon days of infantry attacks and counterattacks. Often, both sides ended up in their original positions. Battles became sieges, the aim simply being to drain the other side's resources. As it became clear that this was static warfare—war at a standstill—leaders began to compute even human casualties like an inventory of shells or fuel. Any loss was acceptable if the enemy loss was greater. In the 1916 battle of the Somme, for instance, casualties totaled more than one million, approximately one man for every four square yards of contested ground.

Trenches became fortresses: above ground—barbed wire, mines, and a maze of foxholes; below ground—command posts, supplies, and damp, rat-infested living quarters. Men burrowed in these places for months, surrounded by corpses and exposed to constant danger from gas and artillery. They hoped to be wounded seriously enough to be sent to the rear for convalescence. Morale grew so bad by the spring of 1917 that mutinies broke out in some French, Italian, and Russian units.

Paul remarks that the trenches are in poor condition. For days his group loafs and makes war on the rats, rats so voracious they devoured two cats and a dog in an adjoining sector. At night the enemy sends gas; by day, observation balloons. Morale is lowered by rumors of tanks, low-flying planes, and flame-throwers. Deafening bombardment continues; the trench is cratered and battered. Food cannot be brought up. One night the men battle a swarm of fleeing rats; one noon a recruit turns into a raving madman from being enclosed in the underground living quarters. That night the dugout survives a direct hit. Suddenly the nearer explosions stop, and the French attack. Paul's company fight and throw grenades and use their sharpened spades like wild beasts, killing to save themselves. The fight continues into the next day, Paul's side chasing the retreating French right into their own trenches. They seize what provisions they can carry and clear out. Back in their own trench, they are too tired even to enjoy their booty—the rare luxuries of corned beef, bread, and cognac.

Night comes, and Paul, on sentry duty, dreams of cloisters and an avenue of poplar trees—quiet dreams in a place where there is no quiet. He believes his generation is lost, unable ever to have innocent peace again. For several days attacks and counterattacks alternate; the dead pile up between the trenches. The men search two days in vain for a crying man. The dead swell and hiss and belch with gas; the smell is nauseating. On quiet nights the soldiers search for souvenir parachute silk and for copper bands from bombs. Two butterflies settle one morning on a skull. Three layers of bodies fill a huge shell hole. Recruits in clothes too big fall like flies; a surprise gas attack kills many. One day Himmelstoss panics and Paul shouts at him until he can grasp an order and regain his wits. Haie Westhus, who had hoped to reenlist in the army for a nice, clean job after the war, suffers a serious back wound. Still, says Paul, they have held their little piece of convulsed earth. It's the only kind of victory to be seen in this war. On a grey autumn night they return behind the lines. Second Company is now down to 32 men.

NOTE: Imagery   Paul again dreams of quiet beauty. He notices a butterfly amid the devastation and comments on how terribly young the replacement recruits are. Of his own group he says, "We are forlorn like children. . . . I believe we are lost." He has felt like a child at least twice before—the night they strung barbed wire and the night he helped Kat baste the goose. Both times he awoke to find Kat there, like a father. Why does part of him long for that element of childhood? What is it from childhood that he thinks he and his classmates have lost so completely?

CHAPTER 7

This chapter gives us some breathing space. We follow the men back to a field depot for reorganization. The change in Himmelstoss seems to be permanent: not only did he rescue Westhus; he has also wangled a job as substitute cook and slips Tjaden some butter and the others, sugar.

NOTE: By this time we could make a list of the ways Remarque has developed his theme: how World War I destroyed a generation of young men. It has taken from them the last of their childhood years, it has destroyed their faith is their elders, it has taught them an individual life is meaningless—and all it has given in return is the ability to appreciate basic physical pleasures. According to Paul, though, the men haven't entirely lost human sensitivity: they're not as callous as they appeared in Chapter 1, wolfing down their dead companions' rations. It's just that they must pretend to forget the dead; otherwise they would go mad.

A theater poster starts a new series of events in this chapter. At the front, or even a few miles behind the lines, dirt and grime and basic survival are the main elements of life. The poster, showing a well-dressed, healthy pair of actors, reminds Paul and his classmates of another world out there somewhere, a civilian world. From history we know that civilians also did not fare well during World War I, but Paul and his friends don't know that; they have not yet gone home on leave. But the poster awakens desires. They try to recover that world in stages. The first stage is simple. They can't do much about their dirty, ragged, clothing, but they can stop the itching awhile—they get deloused. The next stage is better. That evening Leer, Kropp, and Paul dump Tjaden and swim a guarded canal for an evening with three French women. They do the same the next night, carrying the girls bread, sausage, and cigarets kept dry, overhead, in their boots. To us it is clear that the girls are hungry and do not care what uniform a man wears, as long as he's a decent guy and has some food. But Paul wants more; he wants the little brunet really to care about him personally.

One afternoon Paul stands the others drinks: he's been given two weeks' leave plus travel time and temporary reassignment to another camp. He tries to forget which of his friends will still be there when he gets back.

The train trip home provides Paul—and us—with a sense of transition to an entirely different kind of life, as old landmarks appear, even the poplars. He doesn't understand why tears start pouring down his face at the sound of his sister's voice calling to their mother, "Paul is here." Perhaps it is simply homesickness, catching up with him at last. His mother is ill with cancer, and Paul does the most he can for them, offering cheese from Kat and food from his own military rations. In the towns, shortages are acute, though his family has saved Paul his favorite dishes. One day he stands in line at the butcher's with his sister for three hours, but the promised bones are sold out before they can get any. He can't even talk to people any more. If he were to talk about front-line horrors, as another soldier has done, upsetting Paul's mother, how could he stand to go back?

On the whole, the leave he'd wanted so badly is a disaster. After he reports to the district commander, some major whom he fails to salute properly gives him a bad time. To avoid similar situations he changes into his civilian clothes, even though they hardly fit any more. His father and other old men press "the young warrior" with opinions and questions that don't begin to connect with his own knowledge of war. He can't even gain any comfort from the books and papers in his own room.

When he goes to see Franz Kemmerich's mother, she blames him for living while her son has died. In a gesture of kindness, he swears Kemmerich died instantaneously and without pain, but he has seen so many deaths since then that he forgets how he himself felt. He can no longer understand so much grief for one man dead among so many.

The only relief is a visit to his classmate Mittelstaedt, who is now the commander of a reserve unit. To his and Mittelstaedt's delight, Schoolmaster Kantorek is in the unit! He's an absolutely pathetic-looking soldier. Mittelstaedt demonstrates how he humiliates Kantorek and throws his own slogans back into his face. Not satisfied with that, he sends Kantorek on errands with a model reservist, Boettcher, the former school porter, so the whole town can laugh. The scene is comic, yet sad. Even though Paul doesn't blame Kantorek for anything, it's interesting that he doesn't seem to feel the slightest shame at his classmate's behavior. Is this still the same boy who, before his last stint in the trenches, found it sad that the only ambition he had left was to humiliate a mailman?

Finally, the last night of his leave arrives. His mother sits long into the night watching him sleep. At last he lets her know he is awake. She alone has not asked foolish questions. Now she asks gently, "Are you very much afraid?" He walks her back to bed, choked up at her getting him good wool underwear when she is so destitute and ill. He is in agony for what he has lost and for what is happening to her.

NOTE: Shortages   From history we know that in August 1914 the Prussian War Raw Materials Department began stockpiling and allocating raw materials on a priority basis. Civilians weren't high on the priority list. In November 1914 staple foods such as flour and sugar were placed under government control, and in 1915 complete food rationing was introduced in Germany.

CHAPTER 8

Paul goes to his assignment, the training camp near his home town where Himmelstoss "educated" Tjaden. During days of drill, evening of poker and newspapers, he again notices the beauty of nature. At other times he guards Russian prisoners of war in the camp alongside. They are sick and feeble, hanging on to life by picking over the none-too-plentiful garbage from Paul's camp and trading their last few possessions for bread. He loves their courage and their music, and when he guards them he cannot understand why they must be enemies—just because, at some table, a document was signed. As he looks at them, he knows that any soldier would see an officer as more of an enemy; any schoolboy, a teacher as more of an enemy. But he dare not think that way too long, any more than he could tell his family what the front was really like. It's still his job to go back there and kill. But he stores away his thoughts for after the war. He can vaguely see that spreading the truth afterward may be the only good thing he can bring out of this war.

Recall Remarque's introductory note before Chapter 1—is Paul perhaps speaking here for Remarque himself? Could writing this book be a task Remarque set for himself when he fought in World War I? This is at least the second time Remarque has suggested, through his characters, that all men are the same—that only the leaders want war. Recall Kropp's theory for having the right people fight, in Chapter 3.

Paul's father and sister visit him the Sunday before he returns to the front, telling him that his mother is dying and they cannot afford the proper care. At least when it comes to his mother, Paul is not callous: he can't choke down the jam and potato cakes she has sent. He gives two cakes to the Russians and saves the others for his friends.

CHAPTER 9

Paul travels for several days and then loafs, awaiting his company. He is worried about his friends; the company has been designated a "flying division," one assigned wherever the need is greatest. How relieved he is when they return, and Kat, Müller, Tjaden, and Kropp have all survived! The slightly moldy potato cakes serve for a meal of celebration. All are delighted to be issued clean new gear for once, too. But they get to keep the clothing for only eight days of drill and polish—and a visit from the Kaiser. Then it's back to rags. The Kaiser turns out to be a disappointingly small man (like Kantorek and Himmelstoss?) and that leads the friends to a discussion of his power. Would there have been a war if he had said no? Paul says he knows for sure the Kaiser did say no. We know from history that Paul, like many people who are certain, is wrong. Nobody directly contradicts him at this point, but later Kat observes that every grown-up emperor wants his very own war, so maybe the Kaiser figured it was his turn. Meanwhile everyone does agree that if 20 or 30 leaders had said no, there couldn't be a war. Kropp notes how strange it is: everybody's fighting for his own fatherland, sure that he's right. There must be something they are missing. War has always existed; it must be some kind of fever. But that is too philosophical for the others, and it is Kropp who finally growls that they might as well just drop the whole rotten discussion.

Think about Kropp's contributions to all the discussions. How do his ideas differ from those of his companions? Is he as willing as they to speculate that his own leaders might be wrong? What do you think the defeat of Germany will do to his ideals and emotions? Even if he survives, will he be destroyed in exactly the same way as the others?

After Kropp's outburst, a line of white space is our only transition to the next sentence: "Instead of going to Russia, we go up the line again." The Setting section of this guidebook points out the geography: they are going west, to France, despite rumors of going east.

This time they barely notice things that would have horrified them earlier. Bodies, many naked from the concussion of trench mortars, hang in some trees they pass. They casually report the situation at the next stretcher-bearers' post; there's no point getting upset. Back at the front, they volunteer to scout out the enemy position. Paul, separated from his friends in the dark, is overcome with fright until he again hears their voices. He blames his leave; it has thrown his instincts off. But the experience makes him realize that friendship is the one solid element he has left in his life: it steadies him.

In the darkness Paul is pinned down by a bombardment. When a French soldier suddenly stumbles into Paul's shell hole, Paul stabs wildly with a small dagger, hitting the man again and again by reflex. Then, still trapped by the firing, Paul's guilt and horror grow as he bandages the man and waits until he finally dies, about three the next afternoon. He looks through the man's papers and vows not to forget the name: Gerard Duval, printer. He has killed a man, not some abstract enemy. When it is dark again, Paul is able to creep out and find his friends. When he mentions the dead printer the next morning, Kat and Kropp reassure him: "What else could you do?" They point out Sergeant Oellrich, a sniper who boasts about how his targets jump and about how high his kill score is. Paul comments that war, after all, is war.

NOTE: That appears to be the end of the issue. From your own knowledge of Paul, do you think he does forget his vow to make amends? Remarque doesn't tell us; he leaves it open. Some readers think Paul is totally brutalized and that he does forget. Others notice rather that there is just no mention of Duval's wallet and pictures again. What do you think?

CHAPTER 10

By pure good luck eight men, including Paul's "whole gang"—Detering, Kat, Kropp, Müller, Tjaden—draw an assignment that feels like soldier heaven: guarding an abandoned village and supply dump. The only cloud is that by now Haie Westhus isn't with them; he has died even though Himmelstoss had rescued him. Despite some shelling, life near the supply dump means real beds, excellent food, and all the cigars they want. Even when they leave, they do it in style in a big truck loaded with extra food, a canopied bed, two red plush chairs, and even a cat purring in a parrot cage. These wonderful two weeks are the last light moments of the novel.

A few days later, while they are helping evacuate a village, Paul and Kropp are each wounded in the leg. Picked up by a passing ambulance wagon and treated, somewhat roughly, at a dressing station, they bribe their way onto a hospital train going to the rear. Paul hates to haul his dirty body onto the clean sheets and suffers embarrassment over getting a bottle for urination. On the train Albert's fever begins to rise. To prevent their being separated, Paul heats a thermometer to raise his temperature also. His doing so is more than just a childish prank; he and Kropp need each other's presence as much as they need medical care. Put off at the same station, they are also placed in the same ward at a Catholic hospital. The nuns' morning prayers give them headaches till Josef Hammacher takes responsibility for the bottle Paul threw into the corridor, its noisy shattering getting the nuns to close the door. Hammacher says he threw it because he has what is known as a "shooting license," a paper that says he has periods of mental derangement because of his injuries. They also meet Franz Wächter, who suffers such neglect that he dies of a hemorrhaging arm wound, and little Peter, said to be the only patient ever to return from the Dying Room.

Paul's bones will not knit, so he is operated upon. Hamacher warns some new men not to let the chief surgeon try out his pet cures for their flat feet, but in the end they consent. If you've ever been seriously ill or hospitalized, you can understand their reaction; after awhile you'll let the doctor do almost anything, as long as it will get you out of there! Other men come and go; many die. Kropp's leg is amputated, and he becomes silent and depressed, but Paul can finally get around on crutches. At first Paul wonders the wards, doing so just to keep out of Kropp's sight (he doesn't want his friend to feel worse at the sight of his two legs). As he roams, he notices in how many places a man can be hit. The total image stuns him: shattered men in hospitals all over Europe. "It must all be lies and of no account when the culture of a thousand years could not prevent this stream of blood being poured out, these torture-chambers in their hundreds of thousands." He is utterly and completely disillusioned with the traditions and values handed down to him.

After a few weeks Kropp's stump is well healed and he is to be sent off to an institution for artificial limbs. Earlier he would have shot himself, had he been able; now he is more solemn than he was. Even that is quite a change from the hot-tempered arguer we've known. Paul gets convalescent leave. Parting from Kropp is hard, but he tells himself that "a man gets used to that sort of thing in the army." If Paul is so used to it, why is it so hard?

At home, he finds his mother very feeble; this time is worse than his first leave. He returns once more to the line.

NOTE: The Medical Profession   Doctors are dealt a blow in this chapter. They are depicted as cruel, callous, preferring amputation to repair of shattered limbs, and too eager to perform experimental surgery. In the next chapter we hear stories of surgeons aiding the Fatherland by certifying everybody A-1. Each example is undoubtedly based on true cases, but consider also the pressures of mass operations under wartime conditions.

CHAPTER 11

By now Paul has lost a great deal: youth itself, faith in his elders, belief in the traditions of Western civilization. He's even lost much of his own ability to rise about pure animal reactions—to feel and think as a sensitive human being. Only comradeship now keeps him going, and he has already seen several friends killed or maimed. In this chapter Paul records the collapse of the Western Front during the last terrible year of World War I, and the deaths of his few remaining close friends.

It was winter when Paul returned to duty. His life has alternated between billets and the front until it is once again spring. His moods and thoughts depend on the kind of day it is; all soldiers are brothers in this. They have been reduced to relying on animal instinct to avoid death. Otherwise the madness around them would kill them, physically or emotionally. Says Paul, "We are little flames poorly sheltered by frail walls against the storm of dissolution and madness, in which we flicker and sometimes almost go out. . . . Our only comfort is the steady breathing of our comrades asleep, and thus we wait for the morning." Every barrage cuts into this thin protective shell, however; everyone's nerves are dangerously frayed. With Detering it takes only the sight of a cherry tree in blossom to madden him with thoughts of his wife and farm. He deserts but is caught and court-martialed. Another man, Berger, six feet tall and the most powerful man in the company, dashes into a barrage to help a wounded messenger dog. A pelvis wound kills him. Yet another man madly tries to dig himself into the earth with hands, feet, and teeth. Müller is shot

point blank in the stomach. Before he dies he gives
Paul Kemmerich's boots; they are to go to Tjaden
next. (Is this simply being practical, or a premonition
of death to come for Paul?) As the men bury Müller,
they are saddened to think that well fed English and
Americans will probably soon overrun his grave. For
the enemy are sure to win. They are well fed on beef
and bread, well supplied with guns and planes, while
the Germans are emaciated, starved, short of all supplies. For every German plane there are five English
and American planes. For every German soldier there
are five of the enemy. Dysentery is constant, the artillery is worn out, the new recruits are anemic boys
who can only die. Tanks are common now, new and
terrible armored beasts that squash men like bugs.
Things have grown so bleak that Paul is reduced to
reciting lists. The men see only:

> Shells, gas clouds, and flotillas of tanks—shat-
> tering, corroding, death.
> Dysentery, influenza, typhus—scalding, chok-
> ing, death.
> Trenches, hospitals, the common grave—there
> are no other possibilities.

In one attack the company commander, Bertinck, a
superb front-line officer, dies shooting a flamethrower
team about to ignite the oil in his companions' trench.
A final fragment that shatters Bertinck's chin plows
on to tear open Leer's hip. It takes Leer only minutes
to bleed to death. Still the bloody and terrible summer
wears on. Weeks of rain leave rifles caked with mud,
uniforms sodden, the earth an oily, dripping mass.
Tormenting rumors of an armistice make the front
even more unbearable. Then one late summer day,
Kat is hit. Paul bandages his smashed shin and strug-
gles to carry him to an aid station. But there the

medics shake their heads; Kat has died on Paul's back, killed by a stray splinter to his head. Paul reels in shock. How is it that he can see and move—with Katczinsky dead? He faints at this loss, his last and best friend.

CHAPTER 12

Soon it is autumn. Paul has been on two weeks' rest because of gas poisoning. On leave, he sat in the sun listening to news that the Armistice would come soon. But now he is back at the front alone, confronting the future dully, without even fear. Still he believes there is some bit of life within him that will seek its way out.

And then we come to a break in the text. The narration switches to third person—someone else, not Paul, is speaking. The narrator tells us that Paul fell on an October day, an October day so quiet that the army report confined itself to the single line: "All quiet on the Western Front." His face was calm, almost glad. He did not appear to have suffered long.

Our feeling is almost one of relief. In the last two chapters the misery has been so relentless that we are convinced of the hopelessness of the chance that Paul (or any of his friends) could create a good life after the war. The bitter irony is that he should have survived so much terror and died so quietly—only one month before the Armistice.

A STEP BEYOND

Tests and Answers

TESTS

Test 1

1. Remarque's principal purpose in the novel was to _____
   - (A) present a vivid portrayal of the horrors of World War I
   - (B) show how a German generation was affected by the war
   - C. set the record straight about trench warfare

2. Paul and his friends were encouraged to enlist by _____
   - A. the editorials written by Herr Krauss
   - B. the town's leading politician, Heinrich Böll
   - (C) the schoolmaster, Kantorek

3. A symbolic action which points up the war's effect upon morality was _____
   - A. Müller's attempt to get the boots
   - (B) the theft of Kemmerich's watch
   - C. Paul's killing of Gerald Duval

4. In the process of training the young soldiers, Himmelstoss tried to _____
   - (A) break their spirits
   - (B) inspire them with Germany's glorious destiny
   - C. develop their sense of mutual responsibility

5. Katczinsky's great skill lay in his ability to   _____
   A. cut through red tape
   B. scrounge for food
   C. be the best marksman in the company

6. The halfway existence of the soldiers between   _____
   life and death is best illustrated by the scene in
   the
   A. hospital
   B. cemetery
   C. field depot

7. One of the terrible images of the battle scene is   _____
   the
   A. dying horses
   B. bayonet charge by "the gladiators"
   C. suicide of the frightened soldier

8. The theme which is NOT developed in this   _____
   novel is that war
   A. is inevitable
   B. destroys ambition
   C. helps develop brotherhood among the
      soldiers

9. The several references to butterflies in the   _____
   novel
   A. provide a contrast to the horrors of war
   B. are inserted to show Paul's scientific
      interests
   C. introduce Paul's vivid dream sequences

10. Paul shows compassion for Kemmerich's   _____
    mother by
    A. sending her an optimistic letter in her son's
       name
    B. telling her that Franz is recovering
       satisfactorily

C. lying about the manner of her son's death

11. *All Quiet* is sometimes said to be lacking plot and characterization. Is this true? If so, does it harm the novel?

12. In wartime, society seems to suspend the Ten Commandments for soldiers. Explain this idea and use examples from the novel to support your points.

13. All through the war, Paul and his friends seem obsessed with food, comfort, and physical things. Give several examples involving food and comfort and explain how these examples provide an indication of how the war is progressing.

14. Explain the meaning of this statement: "Chance rules a soldier's life at the front." Give examples which support your explanation.

15. Explain why Paul objects to his and his friends' being called "Iron Youth."

Test 2

1. One sign of the deteriorating conditions in _____
   their army was
   A. the substitution of crepe paper for cloth
      bandages
   B. the desertion of many German officers
   C. the making of coffee out of soy beans

2. Paul realized that the difference between his _____
   first and second leaves was that
   A. his family had started to blame the
      Kaiser
   B. the civilians now expected to lose
   C. he had changed

3. "Forgive me, comrade. We always see it too _____
   late" are Paul's words to
   A. the dead Frenchman
   B. the dying Kemmerich
   C. the locksmith, Tjaden

4. Paul's mother, father, and teachers _____
   A. attempt to build up his morale when he is
      on leave
   B. are out of touch with the reality of Paul's
      situation
   C. symbolize the wholesome side of
      Germany

5. Paul's conclusions about the Russian _____
   prisoners of war are that they
   A. are inferior to the Germans
   B. cannot be trusted
   C. are similar to the Germans

6. Paul is unable to understand _____
   A. how both sides can be fighting for a just
      cause

B. why Germany has not been victorious

C. why the Kaiser lied to the troops

7. Paul wonders what will become of his   _____
generation now that

A. "our education has been forever blunted"

B. "our knowledge of life is limited to death"

C. "our morals have been corrupted beyond redemption"

8. Josef Hamacher, the soldier in Paul's hospital   _____
ward, said that war is a glorious time for all the

A. generals

B. munitions makers

C. surgeons

9. A final irony of the novel is that Paul's death   _____
came

A. in a camp accident

B. shortly before the Armistice

C. as he left for home on a furlough

10. On the day that Paul died, the army   _____
communique read:

A. All quiet on the Western Front

B. Our brave forces have repelled a vicious enemy thrust

C. Casualties were light in defense of the Fatherland

11. Using examples to support your points, support or refute Paul's statement, "A hospital alone shows what war is."

12. Using several incidents that occurred while Paul was home on leave, explain why he concluded, "I do not belong here any more, it is a foreign world."

13. Although it is not true, Paul tells Kemmerich's mother that Kemmerich died instantly and without pain. Defend, or at least explain, the motives for Paul's actions.

14. Explain why Paul and his friends believe that the war has ruined them for everything.

15. Using several examples, discuss the vital role played by friendship in this novel.

ANSWERS

Test 1

1. B   **2.** C   **3.** B   **4.** A   **5.** B   **6.** B   **7.** A
8. A   **9.** A   **10.** C

11. This question asks you to do two things: to decide whether *All Quiet* is weaker than other stories in plot and characterization and then to decide whether or not that weakness—if it exists—harms the novel. When you think of stories in which the main characters' desires cause each event, and each event in turn causes the next one, then you must admit that the plot of *All Quiet* is not set up that way. What causes the events in this novel occurs some place in government or the military command, and it doesn't really matter what the characters want. The war will still grind on. In fact, you could rearrange the order of events in the story, or even omit some of them, without really changing the author's message.

    Much the same thing is true of the characters. Although some of them really come alive for us in vivid scenes—the stubborn, red-headed cook; the cruel Himmelstoss; the heroic company commander dying for his men—still, they do not change much in the course of the story, and their wishes and desires do not affect the course of the story. As to whether or not this lack of strong plot and characterization harms the story, you could argue convincingly that it does not. The whole point of the story is to show how World War I tore apart the lives of the young men involved, and setting up the story as a series of events in apparently random order shows exactly how little control they had over the forces destroying them.

12. The Ten Commandments direct people to worship God and to avoid killing, stealing, lying, and adultery. You might begin by restating the first sentence of the question as your topic sentence, and then continue by giving examples of how things usually considered sinful are expected of soldiers. The most obvious, of course, is killing. A soldier must kill to protect his own life. The killing of Duval in Chapter 9 or the mad charge in Chapter 6 would provide good examples. An example of the need for stealing to supplement poor rations could be one of the Kat stories Paul recalls in Chapter 3. A case for lying is Paul's report to Kemmerich's mother of how Kemmerich died. Illicit sex occurs in the evenings with the French girls (Chapter 7) and might be defended as an assertion of life and an attempt to regain elements of civilian life. Society—through the army—even provides brothels for the men! As for worshiping God, the only god the men seem to have is Chance or maybe the Earth itself (see Chapters 4 and 6). In your concluding sentences you might comment on which commandments have to be suspended for physical survival and which ones seem to have more to do with psychological or emotional survival.

13. It's important to read a question all the way through. Note especially the last 13 words of this one: you are expected to relate what you say about supplies and comfort to how the war was going. It will therefore be easier for you to answer if you take your examples from the last few chapters of the book: the conditions at aid stations and hospitals, the unusualness of the supply dump assignment, and, at the front, the scarcity of food, shells, decent clothing, and weapons, especially as compared with the apparently boundless supplies of the British and the Americans. The contrast makes it clear that the better supplied side is going to win. You might also include mention of technological innovations which are simply nonexistent on Paul's side: tanks and flamethrowers, especially, are mentioned in Chapter 11.

14. An obvious response to this question is that pure luck sometimes seems to determine who lives and who dies on a battlefield, that no matter how good a soldier someone is, his skill is no guarantee that he will survive. For examples to support such a statement, you might use the time Paul left his trench to visit another and came back to find it shelled. Or you might use the freak accident which killed Kat at the end of the novel. Review the discussion in this guidebook of the battle chapters (4, 6, and 11) or reread those chapters for further examples.

15. Paul himself discusses the phrase "Iron Youth" in Chapter 2. Reread that section. In your essay, discuss each word of the phrase. First explain why iron is not an appropriate description of skinny boys, either physically or emotionally, and then explain why youth is no longer a good description of the boys mentally or emotionally.

Test 2

1. A   **2.** C   **3.** A   **4.** B   **5.** C   **6.** A

7. B   **8.** C   **9.** B   **10.** A

11. Turn to Chapter 10 where Paul and Kropp are sent to a Catholic hospital behind the lines. After Paul is well enough to move about, he discovers just how many different categories of wounded men are in the same hospital. Find that section and review Paul's ideas. If you agree with Paul, you might simply state Paul's meaning and then support it with figures from history as to how many men were killed, wounded, or maimed for life by World War I. (See the Setting section in this guidebook.) You might also add that seeing all these injuries neatly categorized in a civilian setting—a place where everyone is expected to have full use of his body—makes them seem even more horrible than at the front where you expect injury and death.

    If, on the other hand, you disagree with Paul and think that the battlefield shows more truly what war is, you might use examples from Chapter 6 (the long chapter detailing what an endless period of trench warfare involved) or the screaming horses from Chapter 4. The crying of the horses dramatizes in quite a different way how directly contrary to nature war is.

12. This question takes you directly to Chapter 7 in which Paul goes home on leave. Examples follow one another quite rapidly within that chapter. Ones you might want to include are the major who does not seem to understand anything about war and insists on marching and saluting, and the armchair strategists who tell Paul he couldn't possibly understand the overall picture of the war since he is fighting in only one part of it. Even Paul's mother, who seems more understanding than they, reduces the war to a discussion of how to get a safe job and the need to be careful of French women. In

each example state what happened or was said and show that it is foreign to Paul by contrasting it with the kinds of things he has been experiencing at the front.

13. Paul's lies to Frau (Mrs.) Kemmerich can be explained in several ways, some more flattering to Paul than others. Reread two sections: the end of Chapter 2 where Paul sits next to the dying Kemmerich, and the section in Chapter 7 where he actually talks to Kemmerich's mother. Then decide for yourself which motive is uppermost or whether Paul may have had mixed motives: a desire to spare her feelings, a desire to give Kemmerich's death greater dignity than it really had, the fact that he just didn't care and wanted to get a distasteful job done with the least trouble, or even a revenge motive—to deprive her of the truth because she blamed him for surviving.

14. It is Kropp who actually says, "The war has ruined us for everything." The comment occurs in a discussion of plans for after the war in Chapter 5 and refers specifically to Paul, Kropp, and their classmates. In your answer contrast Paul and his classmates with other soldiers who have jobs or wives to return to. The Characters section of this guidebook will help you review which soldiers have something or someone to go back to. Consider also why it will be difficult for Paul and his classmates to take any job seriously after the war. What has happened to make all ordinary jobs or studies look pointless to them?

15. Friendship is such a constant theme of the novel that you should be able to find examples in nearly every chapter. For a quick review of some of the scenes involving comradeship see the Theme section of this guidebook, and consider also how the classmates' beating of Himmelstoss and, later, the change in Himmelstoss demonstrate different aspects of friendship.

Term Paper Ideas

Papers Based on Chapters of the Novel

1. Chapters 1 and 2: Study the obituary page in a local newspaper. Write a similar obituary for Franz Kemmerich. Use details from the novel for the general facts, and fill in with suitable additional ideas as needed.

2. Chapter 3: Choose Kat's theory of equal pay or Kropp's theory of having the leaders fight the war personally. Argue for or against the theory as being a good way to conduct war.

3. Chapter 3: Discuss the way Paul and his friends took revenge on Himmelstoss. Were they right or wrong to do what they did? (If you wish, you may include a comparison with how Mittelstaedt treats Kantorek in Chapter 7.)

4. Chapter 4: Explain the statement, "To no man does the earth mean so much as to the soldier."

5. Chapter 5: Explain how the goose incident shows that comradeship means everything to the soldier.

6. Chapter 6: Explain either why "every soldier believes in Chance" or why the men must fight "like wild beasts."

7. Chapter 7: Why is leave "a pause that only makes everything after it so much worse"? Consider the words and actions of Paul's family and acquaintances in your response.

8. Chapter 8: Paul guards Russian prisoners of war in this chapter. What does he seem to learn from this experience? What does he seem to have in mind as a possible goal for himself for after the war?

9. Chapter 9: Explain the difference between "heightened caution" and "animal fear."

10. Chapter 9: Contrast Paul's killing of Duval with Oellrich's sniping at the enemy. What makes their actions different?

11. Chapter 10: Write a paper of comparison and contrast based on the men's lives at the supply dump and at the hospital. Include such areas as food, physical comfort, and comradeship. Explain both what was alike in the two situations and what was different.

12. Chapter 10: Find out more about medicine during World War I. Was Paul's opinion of the medical profession justified? (You might also consider a comparison with medicine during the Korean Conflict as shown in reruns of the television series "M*A*S*H.")

13. Chapter 11: Something mentioned again in this chapter is the callous attitude that a soldier must take toward an individual death. This attitude is shared by the orderly in Chapter 2, Paul when he is talking to Kemmerich's mother in Chapter 7, the medical profession in Chapter 10, and the soldiers themselves. Why is this matter-of-fact attitude necessary?

14.   Chapter 11: Study the obituary page in a local paper. Write a similar obituary for Stanislaus Katczinsky. Use details from the novel for the general facts, and make up suitable additional ones as needed.

15.   Chapter 12: Study the obituary page in a local paper. Write a similar obituary for Paul Bäumer. Use details from the novel for the general facts, and make up additional ones as needed.

16.   Chapter 12: How do you feel about Paul's death in the last chapter? What did he have left to live for? Argue that his death was either tragedy or a blessing and explain what led you to your conclusion.

The Novel as a Whole

1.   Explain the symbolic importance of the goose incident in the novel.

2.   Explain the symbolic importance of the screaming of the wounded horses in the novel.

3.   Explain the importance of Kemmerich's boots in the novel. What do they tell you about the historical situation? about the theme of friendship?

4.   Explain the importance of Paul's daydreams in the novel. Are they present merely as a way for Remarque to show contrasts? Do they tell us something more about what happens to a soldier's inner values? Do they have no importance at all?

5. Explain the importance of the earth itself in the novel. Use examples from several different chapters in order to show how the earth is a source both of safety and of pain to the soldier.

6. Discuss the effectiveness of using first person narration in this novel. Why was it good or bad to have that particular soldier—Paul—telling it? Why not Kat or Kropp or Detering?

7. Discuss the author's use of contrasting scenes. How did this make the novel more vivid? How did it make it possible for you to visualize and to feel what was occurring? Use examples from the novel in your answer.

8. Go back to the introductory statement made by Remarque just before Chapter 1. Has Remarque fulfilled the purpose he set for himself? Explain the reasons for your answer.

9. Explain the psychological defense mechanisms soldiers cultivated in order to survive with some degree of sanity. What did they do to keep the war from getting to them?

10. Review the battle chapters (4, 6, 9, 11). List the words using onomatopoeia to describe the sights and sounds, and explain what effect these words have on the realism of the scenes.

11. Paul and his friends have several discussions about war. In addition, Paul's own thoughts go even deeper, to ideas about human nature. List the major conclusions you believe Paul reached about human nature. Use examples of his actions or thoughts to support your points.

First Person Writing

A. Select one of the following situations and become that person. Using "I," write out either your thoughts, or what you, as that person, would have written in your private diary. Be sure to use appropriate details from the novel, but also to make up additional ones suitable to the person and the situation.

1. You are Katczinsky. You have just been given a new group of recruits to take out on their first mission. You are looking at them and thinking about your own skills and luck and their chances of survival.

2. You are one of the three French girls. You are really hungry. You see the German soldiers swimming; they look like decent types. What are you thinking before you wave to them and start talking?

3. You are Himmelstoss, receiving a decoration from the Kaiser. You realize how very much you have learned. You are thinking with shame about how you treated the recruits and how things were at the front. You do not hold a grudge against Paul and his friends for beating you up.

4. You are Detering and you have had it. You are thinking about your life before the war and building up to your decision to desert.

B. Again, select one of the following situations and become the person indicated. Write the letter as that person would have written it, using his or her attitudes and ways of speaking.

1. You are Paul's sister. Write to him about the latest developments at home, now that your mother's cancer entirely confines her to bed and you have the responsibility for the household. What are your worries and concerns? How much are you willing to share or explain?

2. You are Paul. You still have Gerard Duval's wallet and the picture of his wife and child. No matter what Kat and Kropp said, you still feel a need to write to Madame (Mrs.) Duval and tell her how bravely her husband died. No one else can do it, but you want to do it kindly. Will you actually sign your name? Will you tell her you were the one who killed him? Make these decisions and then write the letter.

3. You are Paul's company commander. Write to Paul's family to comfort them after Paul dies on such a quiet day, with rumors of a coming armistice filling the air.

Interdisciplinary Topics

1. If no one had told you that *All Quiet on the Western Front* was set during World War I, how would you have determined what war was involved? More specifically, how would you have known that the novel occurs during the last two years of the First World War? Include in your response political, geographical, and technological allusions.

2. Read also Remarque's novel *The Road Back*. It discusses more fully some of Germany's postwar problems, problems hinted at in *All Quiet*. Trace the relationship of the problems from one novel into the next.

3. It is unfortunate but true that, historically, war has led to technological innovations. List new things first widely used in World War I and locate references in the novel which suggest the human impact of this technology of planes, tanks, poison gas, and so on.

4. World War I is the first war from which we have documentary photographs. Seek out books containing some of this photography, and discuss the probable impact of photography itself on people's reactions to the war.

5. In his ironic poem "War Is Kind," written in reference to the American Civil War, Stephen Crane contrasts the supposed glory of war with its reality. Locate a copy of the poem and apply its stanzas to Paul, his friends, and their families.

6. Locate the poem "Grass" by Carl Sandburg, first published in his 1916 collection, *Chicago Poems*. Identify the wars in which the battlefields mentioned were important, and comment on the tone of the poem: How does it relate to Remarque's view of human ability to learn from war? to his comments on the earth itself?

7. Explain how the two following novels develop the theme of a young man's complete disillusionment as a result of war: *The Red Badge of Courage* (1895) by Stephen Crane and *All Quiet on the Western Front* (1929) by Erich Maria Remarque.

8. Ernest Hemingway (1899–1961) was a contemporary of Remarque's. He too believed that war caused a loss of values. Compare the moral collapse shown in Hemingway's *The Sun Also Rises* (1926) with Remarque's themes in *All*

Quiet (1929). How do the two novels seem to express similar views? How do they differ?

9. Read Ernest Hemingway's *A Farewell to Arms* (1929) and Remarque's *A Time to Love and a Time to Die* (1954). Both are love stories set during wartime. How are the two stories similar? How do they differ?

10. In 1649, Cavalier poet Richard Lovelace wrote of war as a glorious mistress in the poem, "To Lucasta, Going to the War." Locate a copy in an anthology of English literature and cite passages from *All Quiet* that suggest that Paul's elders and teachers still held this romantic view of war as a glorious, honorable pursuit.

11. Wilfred Owen was a very promising English poet killed in 1918 in World War I. His poems were published in 1920. Locate Owen's "Dulce et Decorum Est" and relate it to Remarque's account of the gas attack in Chapter 4. You may include other references to lung injuries such as those in the hospital section of Chapter 10.

12 Thomas Hardy (1840–1928) often wrote about the ironies involved in human behavior. In his poem "The Man He Killed," he sounds a bit like Paul Bäumer. Locate a copy in an anthology of English poetry, and cite passages from *All Quiet on the Western Front* in which Paul or Paul and his friends reach similar conclusions.

Further Reading

CRITICAL WORKS

During the second half of his life, German-born Erich Maria Remarque was an American citizen who spent much of his time in Switzerland. His books were more popular with the public than with critics. Also, he wrote in German and his books were then translated into English. As a result, much less literary criticism—in English—exists on Remarque's books than those of other major American authors. There is no biography of Remarque for the general reader.

Barker, Christine R., and R. W. Last. *Erich Maria Remarque*. New York: Barnes & Noble, 1979.

This scholarly book, which uses sources in German and in English, examines Remarque's life and novels in detail.

Jacobs, Lewis. *The Rise of the American Film*. New York: Teachers College, Columbia University Press, 1968.

Lewis Milestone's 1930 production of *All Quiet on the Western Front* is treated as a landmark in early films with sound.

Schwarz, Wilhelm J. *War and the Mind of Germany. I.* Frankfurt, West Germany: Peter Lang, 1975.

An essay in the book compares Remarque's war novel with the work of other German novelists.

AUTHOR'S OTHER WORKS

Semiautobiographical Novels

The Road Back, 1931 (*Der Weg zurück*, 1931).

It is a time of shortages, profiteering, riots, and extremist politics. Men returning from the front no longer fit—with family, at a teacher's college, in jobs, even in bars or dancehalls. They feel betrayed by their Fatherland.

The Black Obelisk, 1957 (*Der schwarze Obelisk*, 1956).

Political unrest, unemployment, and galloping inflation are facts of life in Germany in 1923. Ludwig Bodmer, a 25-year-old World War I veteran, works for a tombstone firm, tutors, and plays organ on Sundays at an insane asylum. He wanders between the Poets' Club and a local brothel and between a circus girl and a beautiful asylum inmate, finally leaving for a newspaper job in Berlin and hoping to find a purpose in life.

Three Comrades, 1937 (*Drei Kameraden*, 1937).

Times are hard and political factions becoming violent in Germany in 1928, but Gottfried Lenz, Otto Köster, and Robert Lohkamp have each other. Car racing and repair, roses from cloister bushes, Robby's piano playing, constant drinking—and death—are interwoven in the story of their friendship and Robby's love of Patricia Hollmann.

Heaven Has No Favorites, 1961 (*Der Himmel kennt keine Günstlinge*, 1961).

Lillian, eager for experiences denied her for three years in a sanatorium, and Clerfayt, a racing driver, make the most of their threatened time together one spring and summer in Paris, Sicily, Venice, and the Riviera. Set after World War II, but the time seems earlier.

The Emigrant Novels

These novels, set from about 1937 to the mid 1940s, usually feature a non-Jewish German deprived of citizenship for political reasons. He associates with other refugees, some Jewish, some from a variety of European countries, all of them avoiding European police since they have no legal papers. The plots continue the themes of *All Quiet on the Western Front*—brotherhood versus man's inhumanity to man—but the dialogues are tiresome debates on life, love, and politics.

Flotsam, 1941 (*Liebe deinen Nächsten*, 1953).
> The lives of several German refugees crisscross in 1937
> Austria, Switzerland, and France—in cafes, hotels, cus-
> toms offices, jails. Young Ludwig Kern and Ruth Holland
> survive separation, illness, poverty, and detention, to
> hold at last visas and tickets to Mexico.

Arch of Triumph, 1945 (*Arc de Triomphe*, 1946).
> German refugee Dr. Ravic and small-time actress Joan
> Madou meet in Paris in 1938. His illegal status and obses-
> sion with revenge on a German torturer, and her faith-
> lessness, make their love affair a stormy one.

The Night in Lisbon, 1964 (*Die Nacht von Lissabon*, 1964).
> Josef Schwarz tells of going back into Nazi Germany for
> his wife, Helen, and with her surviving detention and
> pursuit by French and German authorities. But she com-
> mits suicide on the brink of sailing for New York rather
> than let her cancer mar their new life. Schwarz gives his
> passport and tickets to a fellow refugee.

Shadows in Paradise, 1972 (*Schatten im Paradies*, 1971).
> Robert Ross, art expert and former journalist, arrives in
> New York on the passport of a dead man. He works ille-
> gally in the worlds of New York art and Hollywood films
> during World War II. He loses his love, the model Nata-
> sha, by returning to Germany after the war for revenge
> (unsuccessful) on a crematorium official.

World War II Novels

Remarque did not himself serve in World War II, and the
novels lack the feeling of involvement conveyed by *All Quiet
on the Western Front*. Like *All Quiet* they do, however, continue the themes of man's inhumanity to man and the value
of comradeship.

Spark of Life, 1952 (*Der Funke Leben*, 1952).
> In a German concentration camp during the last weeks of
> World War II, Allied victories rekindle the spark of life in
> Skeleton 509. His underground movement, including the

Jewish lovers Joseph Bucher and Ruth Holland, thwarts many SS atrocities. Shortly before the Americans arrive, Skeleton 509 shoots an SS man and is killed himself, but Joseph and Ruth survive.

A Time to Love and a Time to Die, 1954 (*Zeit zu leben und Zeit zu sterben*, 1954).

Toward the end of World War II Ernst Graeber, a young German on the Russian Front, goes home on leave only to find his neighborhood destroyed by bombs. In searching for his parents, he is sickened by his growing knowledge of concentration camps and denunciations. He meets and marries Elisabeth Kruse, a former schoolmate. Back at the front he saves four Russian prisoners, but is himself shot by one of them as they flee.

Glossary

The English Translation

Originally published in German, *All Quiet on the Western Front* was quickly translated into English. At times, however, the English is distinctly British. While the words are not difficult to understand, you may feel more at home if you scan the American equivalents:

British English	American English
aeroplane	airplane
civil life	civilian life
garden fete	garden party
in fine trim	in fine shape
mess-tin	mess kit
Mind!	Watch out! Be careful!
motor lorries	trucks
munition-column	ammunition convoy
pub	bar, tavern
queue	line
wireless men	radio operators
wiring fatigue	wiring duty or detail

In the Army

Dixie   Oval-shaped British army cooking kettle (from the Hindi *degshi*, a pot or vessel). The navy equivalent is a fanny.

Frogs, Froggies   The French, from an ancient heraldic device (symbol for a shield or coat of arms) consisting of three frogs.

Johnny   As used in context in Chapter 7 it refers to a Russian. This is similar to an American's referring to Russians as Ivans. Ivan, Johann, and John are the same name in three different languages—Russian, German, and English.

Skat   A German card game played by three players using 32 cards. Bids are expressed in numbers. The winning bidder becomes the player and names the exact variant of the game to be played.

Tommy; Tommy Atkins   Similar to G.I. Joe for an American soldier, Tommy means a British private soldier. (A Jack Tar is a British sailor.) At one time all recruits were given manuals in which they were to enter name, date, etc. The model used the fictitious name *Thomas Atkins*.

German Names: Pronunciation

Feel free to pronounce the names in this novel as they appear. You will have a problem being more precise, since English consonant and vowel sounds are not identical with those in German. For instance, the German sound for the *ch* spelling in the middle of a word is our *k* or *h* after a guttural sound we do not have in English. At the end of a word, *ch* is more like our *sh*. Also, the two dots over a vowel (called an *umlaut*) indicate a vowel sound we do not have in English. "Baumer," for example, would be pronounced BOW-mer, but "Bäumer" is pronounced BOY-mer. Therefore these are approximate pronunciations of some of the less obvious names.

Bäumer	BOY-mer
Behm	BAYM
Boettcher	BERT-cher

Detering	DET-er-ing
Franz Kemmerich	frahnz KIM-er-ish
Franz Wächter	frahnz VEK-ter
Haie Westhus	hi VEST-hews
Hamacher	HAHM-ock-er
Himmelstoss	HIM-mel-shtos
Katczinsky	ku-CHIN-ski
Mittelstaedt	MIT-el-shteht
Müller	MEW-ler
Oellrich	ERL-rish
Tjaden	CHAW-den

The Critics

Many critics have hailed Remarque for writing *All Quiet on the Western Front* so objectively, without a trace of nationalism, political ill will, or even personal feelings. Even when a character's inner world is revealed, it always seems to be that person's inner life—not the author's. In 1929, as noted in this guidebook in The Author and His Times, the Nazis attacked the book not on literary but on political grounds, and a few reviewers accused Remarque of sensationalism. In America, magazine and newspaper reviews immediately hailed Remarque as the new Stephen Crane and his novel as an updated *Red Badge of Courage*.

Academic critics, however, have paid little attention to *All Quiet*. German critics were displeased at Remarque's departure from the intellectualism of traditional German fiction, and European and American critics were put off by its being a bestseller—how could anything so popular possibly be worthwhile?

> Remarque succeeded in transcending his own personal situation; he touched on a nerve of his time, reflecting the experiences of a whole generation of young men on whom the war had left an indelible mark.
>
> —*Christine R. Barker and R. W. Last*,
> Erich Maria Remarque, *1979*.

> *Im Westen nichts Neues* is close to him [Remarque]. It appears to be permeated with sincerity and true compassion. Its tremendous success can hardly be explained otherwise.
>
> —*Wilhelm J. Schwarz*, War and the Mind of Germany, I, *1975*.

> . . . this book is an accusation of the older generation who let loose this terrible catastrophe, this monstrous war. It is an accusation of the generation that preached that service to the state was the highest aim in life.
>
> —*Wilhelm J. Schwarz*, War and the Mind of Germany, I, *1975*.

Anyone who was sufficiently in the thick of it for a long period, on one side or the other, might have written this grim, monotonous record, if he had the gift, which the author has, of remembering clearly, and setting down his memories truly, in naked and violent words.

> —"All Quiet on the Western Front"
> [book review], New Statesman, vol.
> 25, no. 5, 1929; quoted in Barker and
> Last, Erich Maria Remarque, 1979.

This particular scene [the Kantorek incident], told with the malicious glee of an adolescent, is typical of the immature and sophomoric attitude of the heroes.

> —W. K. Pfeiler; quoted in Schwarz,
> War and the Mind of Germany, I,
> 1975.

Remarque is proposing the view that human existence can no longer be regarded as having any ultimate meaning. Bäumer and his comrades cannot make sense of the world at large for the simple reason that it is no longer possible to do so, not just for this group of ordinary soldiers, but for a substantial proportion of his entire generation. Remarque refuses to lull his reader into a false sense of security, into thinking that God is in his heaven and all is right with the world.

> —Christine R. Barker and R. W. Last,
> Erich Maria Remarque, 1979.

[Lewis Milestone's 1930 film All Quiet on the Western Front] was one of the few serious attempts at a realistic approach to the World War. . . . The drama was kept within the bounds of its theme: a critical recapitulation of the slaughter of innocents. . . . Many instances were eloquent and moving indictments of the emotional and physical destructiveness of war: the sequence of the dead boy's cherished boots being taken over by his comrade, and the celebrated closing scene of the hand of the young soldier reaching out from the trenches for a butterfly only to fall limp on being shot."

> —Lewis Jacobs, The Rise of the
> American Film.

NOTES

NOTES